Dealing with Depression

A Whole-Person Approach

Russell M. Abata, C.SS.R., S.T.D.

and

William Weir, Ed.D.

LIGUORI
PUBLICATIONS

One Liguori Drive
Liguori, Missouri 63057
(314) 464-2500

Imprimi Potest:
John F. Dowd, C.SS.R.
Provincial, St. Louis Province
Redemptorist Fathers

Imprimatur:
Monsignor Edward J. O'Donnell
Vicar General, Archdiocese of St. Louis

ISBN 0-89243-170-9
Library of Congress Catalog Card Number: 82-84045
Copyright © 1982, Liguori Publications
Printed in U.S.A.

Cover Design: Pam Hummelsheim
Cover Photo: H. Armstrong Roberts

This book is dedicated to you who are weary and heavily burdened. Only the sensitive of heart can know how much you hurt and need healing.

The authors want to thank all who have in any way contributed to the writing of this book. Their lives — plowed often and deeply by the sufferings of depression — provide the groundwork for our writing. We acknowledge a special debt of thanks to Carol La Plante for her poems that add an appealing, sensitive touch to the different sections of this book.

Table of Contents

Introduction

Have you been feeling so down that even small decisions seem too heavy to make and carry out? Have you begun to avoid others because you worry what they think about you? Have you been trying to carry on externally but internally felt yourself falling apart? Have you spent days with an anxiety that will not go away? Has your mood felt as dark and black as a night without stars?

If you have felt the weight of any of these frightful feelings, you could be slipping in and out of depression. You do not have to be told how horrible you have felt.

What can you do about your condition? Is there something you can do or someone you can turn to for help? Can your family doctor help you? Can a psychologist help you? Can religion help you? Can you do something to help yourself?

Be assured that help is available. The important question is, where? Where can you find the help you need to feel better?

Before you can answer this question with intelligence and some guarantee of success, it will help if you know what you are facing. This book can help you understand what is happening to you. It is filled with practical knowledge about yourself and your depressed condition. Although it is not a complete treatise on depression, it is a competent, adequate treatment meant to show you what you can do to help yourself feel better.

For your convenience, this book is divided into three sections. You can read these sections one after the other; or, if you find it more convenient, you can skip over a section and return to it later. Section one — the first two chapters — points out what depression is. The second section — the next four chapters — shows you what causes depression and how it affects your whole being. The last section — the remaining four chapters — suggests some practical aids in overcoming your depression.

Nothing in life should be wasted, especially pain. Pain is a relentless teacher. Sometimes its teaching is obvious. "I have a toothache." Sometimes its teaching is not so obvious. "I do not feel well." Depression is a pain whose teaching is not obvious. We hope this book will help you understand what depression is trying to teach you, so you can do what is needed to free yourself from it.

So, fasten your seat belt and prepare yourself to take a journey with us. We hope we will be sensitive, skillful guides and that your trip will be a successful one.

Section One
Understanding Depression

A Reason Just to Be

The sun is painted golden 'midst the clouds,
The sky is a curtain hanging by the sea;
One prayer pours forth from within my heart:
Lord, give me a reason just to be.

The blades of grass that crowd about my feet,
The wind that dances swiftly as it goes;
The fickle lives of others that must pass on:
Lord, that only I may know . . . .

To what purpose these days of life are aimed,
And from this struggle what shall come to be;
As the humble blind man begging at your feet:
Lord, that I may see.

Like the waves that rise but slip back to the sea,
The thief of time must steal e're he but gives;
Happiness, laughter, peace and dreams —
Ah! All dies that lives.

Imprison me no longer in this tomb,
Set me upon the path that leads to Thee,
And let me find an end for this unending climb:
Lord, give me a reason just to be.

Chapter One
Depressed or Down?

As you take your first steps into this book, it will help to clear away some obstacles that might block your way.

First, bear in mind that you are not alone in what you are suffering. There are millions of people just like you. Nor are they mostly women. Women exhibit their depression more readily than men, but they do not have a monopoly on depression.

So, you do not have to add the weight of shame or embarrassment to your pain. You are already under too much pressure. You do not need more.

Nor need you feel that life is unfair in picking on you to suffer this way. Some self-pity is normal to every form of suffering. Too much self-pity holds back the process of recovery. So, depression is something that is happening to a lot of people and can happen to anyone.

Second, although they resemble each other, there is a big difference between being *down* and being *depressed*. There is also a big difference in the way they should be treated. Our major consideration in this first chapter will be to explain this difference.

Down feeling

Being down is a heavy feeling that comes over you when you are overtired, confused, or disappointed. Whatever good feelings you previously possessed have drained out of your being. A heaviness has set in, and you can feel yourself going under. It is a terrible way to feel.

What has brought on this low feeling?

It has probably been brought on by complications in your social, emotional, physical, or spiritual life. Maybe someone you trusted has disappointed you. Maybe your emotions are hurting and reacting excessively because you are having a difficult time in feeling them or expressing them. Maybe a decision you made about a business deal has turned out badly. Maybe your conscience has you worried over something you have done or not done. We could make a long list of things that could have gotten you down.

Although they are frightening, these feelings are both normal and natural. They are not to be taken too seriously. Somehow, you will work them out, or they will work themselves out. It would be foolish to think you could avoid them. These down feelings are a part of the difficulties Christ said we would meet each day. " . . . Today has troubles enough of its own" (Matthew 6:34).

These are down feelings. They are rather simple and short-lived.

Depressed feeling

Depressed feelings differ from down feelings. They are not a simple, passing reaction to a misfortune. They are a set of feelings that are so heavy that not even a professional weight lifter can sustain them.

What do they feel like?

You feel as if all life has turned off inside of you, and you cannot think, move, or do anything. Depending on the severity of your depression, you feel like something inside of you has died. Above all, you feel hopeless.

Hopeless — that is the perfect word to describe how you feel. A part of your world, whether it be in the social, emotional, physical, or spiritual areas of your life, has caved in on you; and you feel helpless and hopeless in the situation. You cannot run away. You cannot explode your way out with anger. You are hopelessly trapped. Can someone come to rescue you? No. You do not feel that anyone will be able to help.

That is depression. It is the heavy weight of hopelessness. With down feelings, there is a hope that things will get better. With depressed feelings, there is no hope that things will improve. If anything, you are sure they will get worse. As time passes and you do not feel better, you become solidly convinced of the hopelessness of your position. If that lasts for a period of time, you do not have just depressed moments or moods. You have entered into the state of depression.

To make more clear this difference between these two types of feelings, we will give a concrete example of each. We will also present a questionnaire to help you to determine whether you have down or depressed feelings.

Joseph's complaint

Joseph's negative reactions to his job demotion are an example of down feelings.

Because his parents instilled him with the standards of a "day's pay for a day's work," Joseph always gave a great deal of himself to his job. He worked as if the company were his own, and he felt a financial loss for the company as if it were his own personal loss. It was not because a financial loss threatened his job. No, it was simply because he was so involved.

The boss liked his work and promoted him until he was second-in-command. But one day the boss informed Joseph that he was going to overhaul the company and that a younger man would be in charge.

Joseph was shocked! He was angry at the changes that would take place in the company and angry that a less experienced man would be in charge. What was he to do?

Joseph felt himself slipping. He was hurt. He was tired. His heart was heavy. Silently, he left work that night. He could not remember when he felt so down. His wife sensed his mood as soon as he walked into the apartment. Knowing that he did not want to talk at the moment, she did not say anything. He would talk about it later.

Was Joseph depressed? He certainly looked depressed, but that did not mean he was. That he was down was obvious. But he was not depressed. He did not need the esteem of his boss or his position so much that he felt panic over what was happening. He was hurting, but he knew his hurt would pass. Besides, he was learning a hard lesson in reality. He was learning that a job is a job. It is not your life. In a few days he would be all right.

Jean's lament

Jean's negative reactions to her loneliness are an example of depressed feelings.

A woman in her fifties, Jean finds herself alone. She has a husband, but there is little or no communication between them. She has children, but they are off doing their thing. Her health is good. She has a beautiful home, but its upkeep rests on her shoulders. It is also a prison, because her training has cautioned her that a woman's place is in her home. It is her castle.

At first glance, Jean seems to have so much, and she actually does; but each of her positives has a corresponding negative. It is expressed by the word "but."

Jean feels so alone, and she does not know what to do about it. She is hurt, resentful, bored, and frightened for her future. Although she is filled with panic inside, she cannot admit she needs help. That would be too embarrassing. That would justify what she fears others are saying about her. She has tried drink, but she knows that is no answer. The thought of an affair crossed her mind, but she dismissed it. The truth is that Jean has no answers. She feels depressed out of her mind.

Is Jean depressed or only down? She is depressed. She has no hope of satisfying her need for companionship and understanding. She sees no relief in sight for dealing with her pains of loneliness.

Judge for yourself

Ask yourself, and try to answer honestly, the following questions. Your responses will give you a clearer picture of down or depressed feelings. (The first question of each set indicates down feelings. The second indicates depressed feelings.)

Do you feel low from time to time? Have you felt for a long time that you have been sinking into an empty pit within yourself?

Are you annoyed and concerned by recurring money problems? Do you feel hopelessly trapped in an inadequate financial situation?

Are you hurt when you are neglected? Do you feel you are always left out?

Do you find yourself expressing resentments when things do not go your way? Have you felt that your insides would explode with anger over a stressful situation?

Has another's embarrassing remark cut you deeply? Have you been obsessed with it?

Have you felt overtired when you work extra hours? Are you exhausted from doing next to nothing?

Do you find it hard to pray? Do you find it impossible to pray because you feel that God has stopped listening to your prayers?

Do you think that even though things look bad they will get better? Do you feel they can only get worse?

Your answers to the above questions will give you some indication of whether you are feeling down or depressed. Further helps will be given as you read on.

If you judge that you are down, not depressed, that is worth a sigh of relief. What you are experiencing is temporary; it is not that serious.

Now the question arises — would it be of profit for you to continue reading this book?

We, the authors, feel it would be helpful. Preventive reading is important in all areas of life. Here it could keep you from crossing over the line from down to depressed at a later time. Besides, although the information contained in the remainder of this book is directed at those who are depressed, it is both practical and deep enough to be of value to everyone.

Questions

1. When was the last time you felt the sinking effects of strong negative feelings? Was it recently? Were you down or depressed? What is the difference between the two? Does knowing this difference help you to understand yourself better?

2. Do you know other persons who are heavily laden with negative feelings? Are they depressed or only down?

3. In the following Psalm 102, is King David down or depressed?

> O LORD, hear my prayer,
>   and let my cry come to you.
> Hide not your face from me
>   in the day of my distress.
> Incline your ear to me;
>   in the day when I call, answer me
>   speedily.
> For my days vanish like smoke,
>   and my bones burn like fire.
> Withered and dried up like grass is my
>   heart;
>   I forget to eat my bread.
> Because of my insistent sighing
>   I am reduced to skin and bone.
> I am like a desert owl;
>   I have become like an owl among
>   the ruins.
> I am sleepless, and I moan;
>   I am like a sparrow alone on the
>   housetop.
> All the day my enemies revile me;
>   in their rage against me they make a
>   curse of me.

For I eat ashes like bread
  and mingle my drink with tears,
Because of your fury and your wrath;
  for you lifted me up only to cast me
    down.
My days are like a lengthening
    shadow,
  and I wither like grass.
But you, O LORD, abide forever,
  and your name through all genera-
    tions.
You will arise and have mercy on Zion,
  for it is time to pity her,
  for the appointed time has come.

How do you judge King David's condition? On what do you base
your judgment? Have you ever felt like David?

Chapter Two
Roots of Depression

If you judge that you are depressed — not just down — what can you do about it?

Perhaps the most important point to remember is that there is a cause for your depression: You are not satisfying one or several of your basic needs. These basic needs come from the social, emotional, physical, and spiritual areas of your life.

For some reason, you are terribly frightened because you are not fulfilling one or several of these basic needs. The truth is that you are in a state of panic, and the panic is so devastating that a depression has set in to protect you from it.

This needs explaining.

Depression — protection from panic

Prepare yourself for a shock.

Although your depression is a serious problem, it is not your main problem. In fact, your depression is meant to be a help. It is nature's way of protecting you and giving you a temporary relief from panic.

Whatever it is, the situation you are in is more than you can handle. You have lost control of the situation, and you are losing control of yourself. You feel so helpless and hopeless. You feel like you are being swallowed up.

In an effort to help you, your nervous system has been on super-alert. It has you so tense and ready to do something that you feel an inner turmoil; it seems you are almost ready to jump out of your skin. You may even find it difficult to breathe or speak. Such a sense of doom and rage has taken hold of you that you do not know what to do. You can try pounding a wall, screaming, rushing here and there, attacking or blaming someone who seems responsible — your parents, God, someone — or breaking down and crying. But these do not give you any respite, or they give you only short-term relief. The experience is just too horrible to bear.

This overextended activity of your nervous system has to let up, or you are going to violently explode.

It is at this point that nature steps in and numbs your nerves until you do not feel the panic, doom, and rage. All you feel is that a heavy lid has been pressed down on your feelings. You are depressed.

What has happened to the panic you felt? Has it gone away? No. Although you do not feel the panic and its accompanying intense feelings of doom and rage, it is underneath the depression. Your feelings are in a strange position. They are not as severely blocked off as they would be in a state of shock. They are somewhere between feeling and not feeling. As one lady expressed it, "I hardly felt anything. People died, things good and bad happened around me, and I did not care. I did not feel them."

Panic: the main problem

So your main problem is not depression. It is panic. Your depression is a product of and a protection against panic. It is a turn-off system to keep your nerves from overstraining themselves.

Depression resulting from panic is somewhat like the fever which follows an infection. The presence of fever indicates that your body is fighting a virus or an infection. Of course, it would be better if you did not have the virus or infection; but the rise in your body temperature means you are fighting whatever is attacking you. That is a good sign. However, if the fever becomes too high, it could destroy you. It must be reduced.

19

The same is true of depression. It could destroy you if it goes too far. For this reason, it should be relieved and eliminated as soon as possible.

How you should handle the depression protecting you from your feelings of doom and rage will be treated in the chapters to follow.

What is true of this natural turn-off system of depression is also true of man-made depressants such as drink and drugs. These attempt to turn off your pain by poisoning or drugging your nervous system. If they are not carefully controlled or supervised, they can become more serious problems than the ones you are trying to overcome.

To illustrate this protective nature of depression, we will present the examples of Melanie and Earl. Both were in situations too difficult for them to handle. They were in the state of panic, and depression arose to stop them from feeling its full, devastating effects.

Melanie's melancholy

Melanie is the middle child of seven children. At thirty-two she is an executive secretary to the president of a prominent firm. She is happy and proud of her position.

One afternoon, just before closing, Melanie's boss called her in to tell her that the firm was moving out of New York to a southern location. He had decided to retire early. As for her, she should not worry. Her performance was excellent, and she would be retained.

Suddenly, Melanie felt dizzy and extremely weak. She experienced a certain sinking feeling. With tears rolling down her cheeks, she managed some words of thanks to her boss for letting her know. Nervous and unsure of herself, she made her way back to her desk. She felt so tired and drained.

Once she got away from the office, Melanie felt a little better. When she arrived at her apartment she immediately phoned her parents and friends, but nothing they said brought reassurance. She tried praying, but that did not help. She could not scream. She could not cry. All she could feel was a sick, old fear of falling into a black pit. She was panic-stricken. It was not long after that she became severely depressed.

What prompted Melanie's panic? Was it because she would have to give up her apartment and say good-bye to old friends and familiar surroundings? That was part of it.

But what bothered her the most was losing her boss. He had become like a father to her. Now he was abandoning her.

What was Melanie to do? She could not face the loss of this special attention in her life. She seesawed between panic and rage, love and hate. It was more than she could handle, so depression set in.

Earl's perils

Earl was in his early forties when he went into a state of severe depression.

Because of the conflicts he had seen between his parents and the effects they had on his four younger brothers and sisters, Earl was glad to leave home and join the Army when he was eighteen.

Earl did well in the Army. The uniform, discipline, and sense of purpose made him feel he was a part of something bigger than himself.

Then the Vietnam War broke out, and the new recruits were disgruntled, critical young people. Everything Earl admired was being torn apart, not by an enemy abroad but from an enemy at home. He felt an old ache of panic creep into his stomach. His mind raced to find ways to stop the destruction he saw within and without, but there was no solution. Worried, angry, and weary, he fell into a state of depression.

How did Earl's depression protect him? It helped to deaden the terrible feelings that had come over him. Earlier conflicts in his home had torn him apart. He could not face that conflict then. He could not face it now. All he could do was panic. After awhile, that gave way to depression.

Learning from depression

If you can see that there is a helpful purpose behind your depression, you may learn to avoid a lot of the "hate" traps common to depressed people.

This knowledge can help you realize that your depression is not something that just happened to *you* — and no one else.

Nor is it a punishment. Dreadful as it may be, it is a form of protection.

Without doubt, there should be a better way of dealing with your panic and its accompanying feelings of doom and rage, but you have not found one. As plant leaves wilt in the hot sun to protect themselves, your viscera constrict, becoming sedated and depressed to protect you. This happens automatically. You are aware of what has happened, but you have no immediate control over it. Like pulling away from a hot object, you just do it instinctively.

You may cry out, "Oh, God, why are you doing this to me?" But your depression is not a form of neglect or punishment on God's part. He is allowing you to use your depression as a temporary shelter or protection until you can find a better way to deal with your panic and the situations that have caused it.

This knowledge can also help you understand your lack of success in gathering your whole self to fight your depression. When you fight it, you oppose the very thing that is trying to protect you. If your choice is between suffering depression or facing panic, the depression is easier to handle and is less taxing to your nervous system. So, you do not have to hate yourself as being so weak that you cannot overcome your depression. Something wiser than your conscious mind has taken over until you can develop the inner forces you need to handle your problems or until someone can come and help you with them.

Questions

1. Does this idea that depression is a protection strike you as strange? Would it strike most people you know the same way? It does not seem like a protection, does it?

2. Do you get very upset when something goes wrong? Do you panic and imagine the worst? Can you remember something that set off panic in you recently? What did it feel like? Did it pass away? If it did, was it really as bad as it seemed?

3. Is there someone you can turn to when you feel panic coming on? If yes, does it help? What does the other person do to help you? Is the fact that he or she is there enough to help you?

4. Have you ever felt Melanie's sense of loss and abandonment or Earl's loss of a home? What were the circumstances of your situation?

5. Does knowing that your depression is a protection make you any less resentful toward God, yourself, and others? Has reading this chapter given you a better understanding of depression?

Section Two
Causes of Depression

In the Park

The rose garden was winter-ravaged
And the leafless trees seemed like
Sculptured columns upon the landscape.
The animals in the park were too friendly.
People had been warm and generous to them
And so, they thought the same of me. A squirrel
Came up to me upon a path and stood politely
On his back legs asking for a handout.
"Are you as afraid of me as I am of you?"
I had asked him and he came closer, so I fled.

I had been afraid to be a friend to the squirrel.
Fear of being hurt had turned me away.
I had not given him a fair chance — nor the world
For that matter. I had prejudiced things in
Closeness as cause of pain, so I did not try.

Many winters and the squirrel are gone.
Now fear no longer holds and hinders me.
With much pain and searching I have learned
To meet people and life and time with joy.
The world and I have had a different kind of encounter.
The winters still ravage the rose garden
But the winter within does not ravage me.

Chapter Three
Unsatisfied Social Needs

As we enter the second section of this book, look back over your shoulder to see what we have considered so far.

Your first look reveals that you are depressed because you are in a hopeless situation. That is what makes you depressed rather than down.

However, when you take a second look, you see that your depression is a secondary reaction to your hopeless situation. Your primary reaction is panic. You are so terrified by what is happening that your nervous system cannot endure it too long. After awhile it closes down so you cannot feel very much of anything. Where did the panic go? It is still there, somewhere, but you do not feel it. All you feel is the heaviness of being depressed.

So you are dealing with three facts — a hopeless situation, your primary reaction of panic, and your secondary reaction of depression. They are all bound together. Take away the hopeless situation and you take away the panic. Take away the panic and you take away the depression.

In this section of our book we want to consider the kinds of situations that can frighten you into panic. As we have indicated, a hopeless situation can develop in regards to your social, emotional, physical, or spiritual needs. Since all of these needs are crucial for you and can send you off into panic and depression, we will give each a full chapter. We will start with your social needs.

Remember what we said in our Introduction. If you find that reading any part of these next four chapters requires more concentration than you can muster at the moment, pass over that part and come back to it later.

What are your social needs?

When we refer to your need for others as "social needs" we are not alluding to your need to go to parties or social events. The needs considered here reach into the core of your being. A good part of your well-being depends on *if* and *how* you satisfy such needs. To stress their importance, we are making them our first consideration.

Although most of the equipment God has given you is meant to satisfy your needs as an individual, some very important parts of you are designed for reaching out to others. Your powers of speech, sex, and love are so many bridges to others. You do not have to be alone in this immense universe. That can be lonely and scary. By reaching out and sharing yourself with others, you multiply your joys and divide your fears. Four or six hands can accomplish more than only two. In fact, this reaching out to others has so many benefits attached to it that it has been recognized not only as a need but as a blessing from the very beginning. The author of the first book of the Bible expresses it this way: " . . . It is not good for the man to be alone . . . " (Genesis 2:18).

So, on the positive side, there are many benefits from going out to others. On the negative side, to be isolated from others by circumstances or by choice leaves a big void in your being. We call this void *loneliness*. It is one of the most difficult pains you can experience as a human being, and it was meant to be that way so that the pain will push you back into the mainstream of life. It does not always work that way, but that is the way nature intended that it should work.

Kinds of social needs

In considering your need for others, let us make it clear that the word "need" can have several meanings.

A person's need may consist of total dependence on others. This is the need of a child or of a severely sick or senile person.

A person's need may be one of partial dependence on others. It is a need to have certain dependable persons near at hand. We generally function better knowing that there is someone we can turn to in an emergency.

A person's need may only be one of contact with others in order to stay current. Conversing with and just being with people help us to dress and conduct ourselves in ways we would probably neglect if we lived as hermits.

Or a person's need may be a desire to know and share with another. This is more a case of "wanting" than "needing." Others help us extend ourselves beyond the shores of self or personality.

Obviously, although all of these persons have a need for others, there is a big difference in what the word "need" means in each case. A person who needs people in the sense of "total dependency" may think it odd that others can stay away from people for a length of time. "Oh, they are crazy! Everyone needs people. There is something wrong with a person who doesn't." What such a person does not see is that the way we need people can make a big difference in our lives. If we freely choose a way of life where we can be away from people from time to time — in order to be more in touch with ourselves and perhaps appreciate people more when we are with them — that can be a good thing. What is healthy for one might not be healthy for someone else.

Healthy ways of relating

What is a healthy need for others?

A healthy need for others is not something absolute or fixed. It depends on where you are in a particular time in your life.

If you are a child or a complete invalid — physically or emotionally — it is healthy for you to be totally dependent on others. Not to have anyone you can depend on so totally is enough to keep you in a state of panic. If you have no trustworthy person with you, you sink into depression.

If you are not a child or a complete invalid, in general it is not healthy to depend on others to do for you what you can do for yourself. Such a dependency puts a burden on you and on others. Obviously, it is not always easy to know how much you need to depend on others to help you. Despite your fears, you should try to do as much as you can to help yourself.

The main point to remember here is this: You need people. If you are in a depressed state, you tend to stay away from people. You are embarrassed or you find it annoying or fear-provoking to be with people who do not understand you or your condition. That is understandable, but it is not healthy. Having people, a number of people, who can each contribute something to help you is the best thing for you. Diet, exercise, activities, and recreation can help you in your depressed state; but they work best when they are performed with others. As life has no good substitute for love, it does not have a good substitute for people.

Unhealthy ways of relating

What is meant by unhealthy ways of relating to others?

To rely on others when you are *able* to rely on yourself is unhealthy.

There are many unhealthy ways of relating to others. Books have been written on the various unhealthy game patterns a person can use in relating to others. For our purposes, we will point out three unhealthy ways.

One way is to take or demand from others what they cannot give. Thus, daily talking for hours on the phone with a friend until your self-esteem has been raised to an acceptable level or until you feel free of a fear or guilt that has been bothering you is unhealthy. Your friend might be able to take on the burden of such heroic listening for a time, but eventually he or she will not be able to put up with it. You will probably need to turn to professional help to resolve your needs.

A second unhealthy way is to stay so small in your feelings and thinking that you rely on others to do everything for you. You feel more secure if others do it for you. You would panic if you had to do it yourself. Thus, you are not willing to take even the smallest chance or risk. You would rather stay where you are in your development than expose yourself to the dangers of change.

A third unhealthy way of relating is closely connected with the second. You try so hard to please others, to win their approval, and to avoid their disapproval that for all practical purposes you do not exist. You have imitated or put on their personalities.

Image living

Another way of expressing this third unhealthy way of relating is demonstrated by those persons who copy a picture *of* themselves and *for* themselves from the actions they see in others.

Take Joey, for instance. His parents made it known that he was to be good and honest. He was rejected if he was not. Teachers praised him when he was smart. They embarrassed him if he was not. The clergy wanted him to be unselfish and heroic like the models they held up for him to follow. He would be eternally punished if he was not. And it was not long before he realized that being attractive was a desirable quality. Others did not make a big fuss over people who were not.

Working with these qualities and depending on how much they were emphasized, his imagination put together a picture or "image" of himself that would win him acceptance. That image, supported by the praise or punishment that encouraged him to put it together, would be the point of reference for all his actions. Because he had not developed a personality of his own, that image would exercise an important influence on him and the opinion he thought others were forming of him. If he lived up to that image, he felt safe, even important. If he did not, he felt unsafe and nervous.

If this image has been formed to win the approval of people who demand perfection, then to buy the wrong shoes, to be taken advantage of by people, or to make a poor choice of a job means deep trouble. With such an image there is no room for failure or imperfection. He can almost hear his parents, teachers, or clergy saying that if he had tried harder, he could have acted better. If someone he knows has acted better, he finds that almost impossible to live with. He must be *number one* or he is nobody.

Dangers of image living

So, if your controlling image demands perfection in relating to others, yours is an unhealthy way of relating to others. As we just saw, it puts impossible demands on you. You cannot make a mistake, take a chance of being embarrassed, get too close to anyone because that one might see that you are not so perfect. Besides, the need to be *number one* provokes such jealousy and competition that it is too painful to even try to relate to others.

All this leaves you in a constant state of turmoil. Even when you feel you have made the right choice or done a thing well, something in this imperfect world will go wrong and spoil it. As Murphy's law states, "If something can go wrong, it invariably will." It seems to go wrong more often for you than for others. Once again you are not good enough. You do not say that *it* is not good enough. No, you feel that *you* are not good enough. You have been called "stupid," "wrong," and "ridiculous" so often by your image that at times you might feel that these adjectives are your real name.

Unfortunately, when something does not turn out perfectly your image pressures you to do it over and over again until it does. If that something concerns religion or conscience, it puts even more pressure on you to do it perfectly or to suffer guilt. Obviously, following the lead of such an exaggerated image, you are continually only inches away from the kind of panic that causes depression.

Further dangers

What is most detrimental about trying to follow such an out-of-control image is that it teaches you, consciously and subconsciously, to judge everything according to what others would think. And, because you are concerned with what they will think, you only have to please them. You do not have to judge things as they really are; rather, you judge them according to appearances. If a thing looks good, it is acceptable; if a person looks good, he or she is acceptable; if you look good, you are acceptable.

As long as it passes the inspection of others you are safe. If it does not, you are in trouble. You become nervous and defensive. You become anxious and worried. "What will people think of me?" shoots across the horizon of your mind. All the embarrassing moments of the past become present there in tension and pressure. You have to get away from them and promise yourself never to be in that kind of situation again.

So, others become your mirror. You can be shallow or hollow on the inside, but if you look good, or what you do looks good, most will not notice. You can bluff your way. Of course, having money or possessions that others want or find desirable helps to cover for shortcomings.

Assuredly, this is not a very satisfying way to live, but it might be the only way you know. Besides, it is hoped that you are not under the domination of such an out-of-control image. Most likely your image is demanding, but it is not so impossibly demanding as described above.

Some guidance from Christ

It might be useful to remember here that this problem of relating to others by way of an overdemanding image is not something new. Unfortunately, it is as old as the human race. It is the reason why Cain killed his brother Abel. It is the reason why the Jewish leaders had Christ condemned to death. He reprimanded them because they did things for "show." He embarrassed them in public by

33

calling them hypocrites. "Woe to you scribes and Pharisees, you frauds! You are like whitewashed tombs, beautiful to look at on the outside but inside full of filth and dead men's bones . . . hypocrisy and evil fill you within" (Matthew 23:27-28). Remember, these people represented some of the best elements of the Jewish community and religion, and yet they had not absorbed the spirit of real personhood or real religion.

Here is what Christ has to say about this unhealthy way of relating to others. In his key address that we call the Sermon on the Mount, Christ says, "Be on guard against performing religious acts for people to see . . . When you give alms, for example, do not blow a horn before you in synagogues and streets like hypocrites looking for applause . . . When you are praying, do not behave like the hypocrites who love to stand and pray in synagogues or on street corners in order to be noticed . . . " (Matthew 6:1-2,5).

Again he cautions against the dangers of trying to relate to others solely to impress them. He inveighs against self-righteousness and judgment of others to lower them and elevate one's self. He says, "Why look at the speck in your brother's eye when you miss the plank in your own?"(Matthew 7:3)

Loneliness

Taking Christ's advice, you will find it helpful to be aware of this trap of doing things *mainly* for show or to impress others. It puts you under too much pressure, and it treats others as if they were things.

How can you tell if you are acting this way?

Let's suppose that you become *excessively* tense because company is coming or you have a meeting with someone important or you are doing everything in your power to avoid someone with a cutting tongue. Some nervousness is understandable in such circumstances, but excessive tension is harmful. It not only makes you want to stay away from people rather than suffer such pressure, it makes you feel very much alone when you are with them. It seems you are speaking and acting in a hollow space. You feel like an actor or actress on a stage of your own. You feel like an island surrounded by noisy people. You have not really enjoyed others. You have performed for them, and you hope you get good reviews for your performance.

So, under this kind of social pressure you feel alone when you are with people and you feel lonely when you are not with people. And the exaggerated, too demanding image by which you judge yourself makes you feel embarrassed in both cases. "What is wrong with you?" it chides. "Why are you that way? Do you think it does not show and that people are not talking about you?"

With all this biting tension, it is no wonder that this kind of loneliness is such a devouring monster. Strangely, it seems that your loneliness is a result of others neglecting you. In reality, you are avoiding them. The possibility of rejection is more than you can risk.

The harmful effects of being overconcerned about what people will think of you are obvious. But let us look more closely at this unhealthy way of relating when it happens in families, with friends, in marriage, and in satisfying social commitments.

Your family relationship

Family is the gathering place where most satisfy their need for people.

When you relate with ease and assurance of acceptance to a father or mother, uncle or aunt, older or younger brother or sister you have someone who makes you feel wanted and not like a burden or a pest. You are wanted because you are you. Even if the other cannot or chooses not to do anything else for you, and even if you are too upset or too worried to appreciate it, his or her acceptance without strings is precious. It lets you know that someone finds you worthy of acceptance. Returning often to such persons is reassuring. You can lean on their acceptance while you clear away the darkness in front of your own eyes — that darkness which has been preventing you from seeing your own worth.

"But in our society, where so many things take me away from home, how do I keep such vital contacts alive? I am sure if I were home with loved ones I would not be so depressed. But I am not. What do I do?"

This is a difficult problem for many, but not an insurmountable one. Our modern age has a remedy for the problem it has created. There are the fast service contacts of phones, letters, and the option of returning home from time to time. Of course, the fastest service of all is to return in thought to those who care. These are not perfect answers, but they can help.

But if no one in the family accepts you as you, there is no returning home. You have a place where you once lived and people to whom you are related, but they do not make a home, at least not a home where you feel you belong.

This is especially true of a family trying to climb the elusive ladder of social success. If you have been plagued with a lack of success, this can be most embarrassing to your family and to you. Your desire to return "home" can be filled with such mixed feelings that you almost prefer to stay away. To have them call attention to your depression and to listen to their preaching to you about it only makes you feel more depressed.

Your relationship with friends

Another answer to your social needs is friendship. If your family does not accept you, because you have not lived up to their expectations, it is hoped that a good friend will. After all, you do not choose your family, but you do choose your friends.

What is a friend? Who is a friend?

A wise man once said, "My friend is my other self." I want for my friend what I want for myself. That almost sounds like Christ's golden rule: "Treat others the way you would have them treat you . . . " (Matthew 7:12).

What do you want for yourself or what do you want your friend to do for you? A friend is someone who thinks of, understands, and accepts you. It is up to you to grow and be worthy of your friend's acceptance. Your friend wants you to do the same for him or her. That is what a true friendship wants most of all. Material or financial help is a secondary consideration.

Having at least one good, mature friend, you have answered your basic social needs. You are never really alone. Having several such friends, you are rich.

How do you find good, mature friends? You have to go beyond appearances to the heart of others. If they can care about you because you are you, they are mature enough to be good friends.

So, genuine friendship is not using people to feed your self-esteem. Keeping a network of people on call to help you feel important and popular is better than not going out to people at all, but this should not be confused with friendship. When such a network breaks down you feel lonely and become depressed. You look around for others, and they are not there. If you are so heavily invested in others, your stock market crashes and you feel worthless.

But with a real friend you are never really alone. Your friend is only a thought away.

Your marriage relationship

Another way of satisfying your social needs is through your marriage relationship.

Subconsciously, marriage partners see in each other a resemblance to a loved mother or father or an ideal loving replacement for an unloved or absent mother or father. Thus they begin their married life. Each partner is like an excited explorer who sees in the other the promise of a very special relationship.

If the promises and vows of marriage are maturely taken and given, the two enter into a friendship that carries a very special pledge of mutual support. They belong exclusively to each other. Although they can and should share their love with everyone, they reserve their sexual expressions of love for each other.

So, marriage can be a most fruitful way of satisfying your social needs.

But what if the partners in a marriage are not mature enough to make such a commitment? What if, instead of being concerned about the good of each other, they are more concerned with showing up other members of the family — having a beautiful home in a swank neighborhood, a well-paying job, and huge success in the social life? What if one partner constantly "puts down" the other, and — instead of being cooperative — one competes against the other? The result of these "what ifs" is often depression.

Obviously, such a marriage is not going to satisfy your social needs. If anything, it creates problems. This is why many have challenged the whole idea of marriage. Fortunately, most persons recognize that it is not marriage that is at fault. Rather, the fault is with the immaturity of those who enter such a marriage.

Your social commitment

A fourth way of satisfying your social needs is by means of social commitment to others.

The word "society" comes from the Latin word *socius*, which means an ally. Each member of society is an ally to others, no matter who they are. When someone in a society is wanting, sick, frightened, or neglected this fact affects others. Immediately, anyone who is incapacitated as a person is incapacitated as an ally. From a long-range point of view, anyone who is desperate for a long time is a potential enemy. Such a person has nothing to lose.

How do you answer the social need you have to improve the quality of humanity? It can be done at the personal level and at the community level.

On the *personal* level, your attitude makes the difference. Everyone is to be judged on how he or she acts as a person. The quality of another's physical appearance, clothes, or speech is not a good basis for judging another.

How much you will help another who is in need of moral or material support should be determined by how much it will really help. In our big cities, there is not much you can do as an individual to help the down-and-out. Consistent community help is needed in that area.

On a *community* level, you should be open to the needs of others. The kind of help you can give will depend on your individual capacity. Whatever you give should not interfere with the care you should take for your own needs. If you neglect your own needs and, then, need others to come to your rescue, you have defeated the purpose of helping others.

So, although these norms are very general, they do indicate a need for you to be on the lookout for others. Never going out to others in need is to close yourself into a very small circle. This does not of itself cause depression, but it makes you so conscious of yourself that if anything goes wrong you can get depressed over it. Besides, when you see others in their need you begin to realize that you are not alone in your personal distress and that your sufferings are not as bad as the sufferings of others.

Gains and pains

Although these four ways of relating — in the family, in friendship, in marriage, and in social commitment — require a much larger treatment than we have given, we hope that each illustrates the two themes of this chapter, namely, the gains to be sought and the pains to be avoided in regards to your social needs.

When you fulfill your social needs properly your gains are obvious. Others can add so much to your life. A word of praise, a word of encouragement, a word of understanding — these make you feel good and worth something because another thinks you are.

This is beautiful. So, you and others should be generous in giving and gracious in receiving praise. It is tragic to see how sparingly families, friends, and marriage partners can be in giving praise. The norm for praising is set so high that praise is seldom given.

"But, is it not a sign of pride or vanity to seek and enjoy the praises of others?" By no means. Pride or vanity is evident when you pretend before others to be more than you are. Praise is simply a recognition that you have been wonderfully made and are capable of doing wondrous things.

In your effort to avoid pain, it is important to realize that everyone wants the approval of others. There is no sense in denying it. So, as often as you can, without going overboard, try to win the acceptance of others. Ordinarily, to say that you do not care what others think of you is not healthy. You will always care what others think of you. You might not be able to act according to what others want, but you will care, even if you say you do not.

But if your social pressures are more than you can handle, you will need to reduce them to a realistic size. An unrealistic "image" of yourself will only drive you away from others. It will deprive you of the benefits you could gain from being with others and feeling wanted, and it will force you into a state of panic as you worry what others are thinking of you.

Signs of unhealthy relationships

Because it is difficult to know when your concern about the approval of others is excessive, here are some signs or guidelines for you to follow. Remember, they are only possible indications of when you are going overboard in your dealings with others. They are given to help you, not to upset you.

- Having a tense feeling of panic in the stomach area when you have failed to impress others or have embarrassed yourself.

- Worrying weeks in advance about a family gathering or party you have to attend.

- Being beside yourself because you are going bald or are showing other unattractive signs of gaining weight or having wrinkles.

- Having a nervous smile or laugh when you say something about yourself that is not becoming or acceptable to the "image" you want to show others.

- Never wanting to speak up because you are shy and afraid of making a mistake.
- Feeling extremely elated when you have shown yourself superior to others or having a sinking feeling of doom when you have come off inferior.
- Never allowing yourself to cry, get angry, or show affection in public because such actions do not look right.
- Playing the game of boastful competition at a group gathering and trying to be the most popular person there.
- Always making excuses to others and yourself as to why things have not worked out.
- Being acutely jealous of another's looks, charm, intelligence, family, and success. Constantly gossiping about the failure of others.

Incentive for change

If, after reading this chapter, you realize that you have been using unhealthy ways of relating to others, do not be discouraged. You can change. The first step away from these unhealthy ways and the depression they have caused is to realize you have been using them.

For now, it is enough to understand that relating to others by way of an overdemanding image is not going to work. It is too critical. It provokes too much anxiety and panic in you. It has you always looking away from yourself and your legitimate needs to what will impress others. It has you on stage all the time. If others accept you, you remain uncertain whether their acceptance is real. If they do not accept you, you are deflated.

So, much of your work in this area of satisfying your social needs is to develop a workable image. It is important to please others and want their approval, but at what price?

A major part of your task is to stand back and realize that it is good to consult your image or what others want of you; but remember that your image is not your real personality, your real self. It is an important source of information telling you what others feel and think is best for you. It is up to you to listen and then make the final decision of what is best.

If you can at least partially understand this and start to work right away, you are on your way out of your depression. (We will consider this more at length in another section of this book.)

Here are two examples for you to consider.

Anthony's obsessions

Anthony is a dynamic professor in a community college in the suburbs of a large city. He is fifty years old. His extended family consists of his father, two older brothers and an older sister, some aunts and uncles. His mother died shortly after he was born, along with a twin brother who died at birth. Anthony has been married twice, but he lacked the constancy to make either marriage last.

While he is teaching and his students listen intently about what they can and must do to save the world, Anthony is fine. He is happy and excited. His students like him and he likes them. He is considered the best professor on campus. That is while Anthony is teaching.

When he returns to his apartment off campus a terrible loneliness overcomes him. On the days he is teaching he can handle his loneliness, but when he has a few days off it becomes unbearable. He misses his family terribly, and when he cannot bolster his self-esteem by impressing people he seems to melt away to nothing. He cannot stand the utter destruction that appears imminent. "A drink will help," he tells himself. "I'm going to get drunk and really feel better. That will do it."

After a few drinks he no longer feels guilty over the long-ago deaths of his mother and twin brother. He visits the neighborhood bars and buys drinks for all who will listen to him. They all agree, their glasses held high, that the world needs saving. When the last bar has closed, Anthony returns to his apartment and calls people to help him save the world.

Anthony, although he is not the ordinary depressed person, suffers terrible panic when he does not have people to relate to and impress. Like a lot of professional people, he needs people to help him feel important. When they are not present he loses himself, his social self. He is paralyzed and lost without it. He feels like a little boy in oversized clothes.

Shirley's phobias

Shirley is an attractive woman of twenty-six. She has two children. Joe, her husband, teaches school and has a part-time job as a shoe salesman. Except for Sunday, Joe is not too visible around the house.

Although she is so young, Shirley has been depressed off and on for a number of years. She is afraid to travel by subway or take a bus or car that has to cross over a bridge, and travel by airplane is out of the question. Actually, she would rather stay home and not travel at all. She is never sure of herself in a crowd of people. She tells herself that she does not care what others think of her, but she knows she does.

What can be said about Shirley?

Despite her appearances of being an adult, she often feels like a small person. This is especially true when she has to be with more than one or two people. She begins to panic. How will she be able to perform well and please so many? The same happens on subways, bridges, or airplanes. She is in panic because if something bad happened how would she act? If she became hysterical, how would she ever live it down?

Unfortunately, Shirley does not see people as allies. She sees them as enemies. She is afraid of their criticism. If someone were to reproach her, she would not know how to handle it. Because of this she looks for and finds all kinds of reasons not to be with people. This depresses her. Fortunately, she has an old school friend she can talk to. She meets her on occasions, and this helps her feel less abnormal.

What about her husband Joe? Is he a help to her?

In a negative way, his absence from home is a help. Not seeing him, she does not have to be reminded how well he gets along with others. Besides, he is so people-saturated by his activities that when he comes home he does not need her to fuss over him and commend him for his work. On the positive side, he does not do much for her. Although he is not a mean or cruel person, he likes her to be shy and always at home. He is pleased with this decided edge: She needs him more than he needs her.

Questions

1. Do you feel that you are depressed because there are not enough people in your life? How do you relate to people? Do you need people because you do not feel you can take care of yourself for too long a period of time?

2. Are you relaxed or on edge when you are with others? With what kind of people are you relaxed? With what kind are you on edge? Do you have someone particular in mind in each case? What is that person like? Do you feel it is better to be with or without people?

3. How can you take on another's personality? If you always do everything someone else wants, does that mean you have taken on that person's personality? Are there times when it is healthy to follow another's lead? Are there times when it is unhealthy? What are some unhealthy ways?

4. What are some of the advantages of having made an image of yourself based on the demands and expectations of others? What are some of the disadvantages?

5. Christ spoke about being "gentle and humble of heart" (Matthew 11:29) and he warned that he "who exalts himself shall be humbled and he who humbles himself shall be exalted" (Luke 14:11). Do you think he knew the dangers of an exaggerated image and how it can get out of hand and make you strive for goals that

are too lofty for any human being? Could he also have had in mind how lofty and self-righteous persons can feel when they have lived up to every detail of their image?

6. How does embarrassment add to the sting of loneliness?

7. Do you have a family you can relate to? Do you feel your family has been supportive in your time of need? How have they helped you? In what ways could they help you more?

8. If you are married, has your marriage helped to ease or to increase your depression?

9. What about your friends? Do you have at least one good friend who really cares about you simply because you are you?

10. Do you walk away feeling that you are "great" because you have helped someone who is down-and-out? Has taking the time and taking a good look at another in need made you feel more humble and grateful for what you have?

11. Are you a "people-worrier"? Are you always worried about what the neighbors, family, people at work, or your friends are thinking about you? When you are about to make a decision, is it harmful to recall what others might say? Can that be helpful as a guide? When does it become harmful?

12. Do you go overboard in buying Christmas, birthday, or other gifts to win the praise and esteem of others and to quiet the needs you have to impress others? Do you give praise generously? When was the last time you praised someone? What did he or she have to do before you felt like bestowing the praise? Can you receive praise graciously?

13. How does relating to others by way of an overdemanding image push you to be popular and, at the same time, urge you to stay away from people so they cannot find out what you are really like? Isn't that impossible, or at least confusing?

14. What do you think of Anthony and his obsessions? He seems to thrive best with a lot of people. Do you think he really gets close to any of them?

15. What about Shirley? She seems to do best away from people. Do you think in her heart that she really wants to stay away or be so scared of people? Are you like Shirley? Do you know people who are so frightened of their performances that they cannot take an elevator or do things where they are doubtful of the outcome?

16. Do you feel that this chapter has helped you to better understand one of the biggest causes of panic and depression? Did you realize that a constant worrying about what people think of you could be so devastating? Can you see how such worrying can deprive you of the benefits of being relaxed with people? Can you see it as a principal cause of loneliness?

Chapter Four
Unsatisfied Emotional Needs

If the unhealthy, "inflated" image you have formed for yourself is making you depressed and is costing you more than it is worth, most of the price is being paid by your emotions. They are constantly on the ledge and edge of panic.

They have no freedom to exist if they are not "nice" or acceptable feelings. They must manufacture the kind of feelings appropriate for every occasion — from crying to laughing to being serious. They must find a way to bear the stress and fatigue of trying ever to maintain your image, despite its demands. They must give you vitality and yet contain themselves within the rigid outlines that are favorable to your image. They must present themselves with the dignity of a statue, move you with the precision of a machine, and yet make you warm, real, and ever-loving.

Obviously, such a strict control on the part of an overdemanding image is one of the main reasons why your feelings are subject to panic and depression. Not only does a need to meet such high expectations increase your fears, the suppression of the strong feelings that could help you cope with your fears leaves you powerless. What is left but panic and depression?

Our goal in this chapter is to examine in detail how your emotions work and how a poor handling of them contributes to your depression.

How your feelings work

Everyone has feelings. Even when you say you feel nothing, you are feeling something. You might not have strong or happy feelings, but you have feelings.

How are they defined?

Your feelings are bodily reactions to things you know. If you like what you see, hear, or touch, your feelings draw you toward it. If there is dislike, your feelings warn you against it.

Your feelings and emotions are intimately connected. The word "feelings" describes whether you like or dislike something. "That is the way I feel about it." The word "emotions" indicates whether you are moving toward or away from what you like or dislike. "I want it. I'm going after it." "I hate it. I don't want any part of it. I'm going to run away from it as far as I can."

It is by way of your feelings that God insures your survival. To help keep you alive, he has put enough "likableness" or pleasure in the things you need and enough "dislikableness" or pain in the things you need to avoid. (This same kind of faculty has been given to animals.)

So, although their pulling and pushing can be confusing, your feelings are important to you. Like critics of food or cinema who report on the menus or movies in a particular restaurant or theater, they give you their reports about likes and dislikes. These reports are neither morally good nor bad. Their purpose is to provide information on how things are in terms of pleasure and pain.

Feelings need freedom

Just as reporters work best when they have free access to all the facts, your feelings work best when they are allowed to be natural and free in making their reports on what is likable and what is not. This is a fundamental need.

It is better, then, to know how you honestly feel about something or someone — even if the information is painful — than to tamper with your feelings until they can give you a favorable report. Persons who allow (or even force) their feelings to lie about or pretend not to see the reality of a situation are distorting some of the most delicate, valuable equipment God and nature have given them. They will never really succeed in such efforts, but their attempts to falsify the reports of their feelings will cause much harm.

Thus, it is not healthy to have your parents or some authority figure tell you that there is no problem at home, on the job, or on a national level when you feel there is one. Nor is it healthy to cause you to feel shame about your feelings. "Oh, how disgusting, how selfish, how terrible you are for feeling that way!"

Your feelings need to be free to have and make their reports, at least to you. Whether you will express their reports to others or whether it is wise or moral to act on their reports will depend on what is good for you as a whole person. You are not just your feelings. There is more to you than that. *You* have feelings. You are not your feelings. Other parts of you need to make their reports before you can make an intelligent, *whole*some judgment on what to do.

Objections

You may find this difficult to accept. "I have a number of difficulties in taking such a position with my 'less desirable' feelings.

"How do I arrive at this kind of freedom if I have never known it? How do I deal with my family members and religion teachers who labeled anger, jealousy, and hate as not acceptable or sinful? The image I have formed of what a good person is like would never let me tolerate such feelings. There would be a constant civil war going on, and I would feel, at best, tired, at worst, guilty.

"Besides, how do I handle my 'undesirable' feelings? What do I do with my fear? How can I turn such a feeling loose within me and deal with it? Isn't it easier not to let such a feeling exist?"

These objections or difficulties about allowing your feelings the freedom to exist and make their reports known to you are valid and understandable. We are dealing with things that are not easy to grasp or control. But let's take a brief look at these difficulties.

First, if, in the past, you have not allowed all of your feelings freedom to express themselves, prepare now to become more aware of them. All of your feelings are operating within you, so take the time to notice them. Once you get into the habit of doing this, you will find it easier to give your feelings their freedom.

Second, if your difficulty arises from your family members and religion teachers who have confused *having* feelings with *acting* on them, you have a problem. They feared, and often rightly so, that if you had a feeling you would act impulsively on it. Rather than allow it to gain control over you, they thought it better that you deny the feeling altogether. (Later, we will examine less harsh or destructive ways of controlling your feelings.)

It is better, then, to have your feelings and listen to them. The cost of repressing them and the loss of positive power that your negative feelings can generate is enormous. Also, the side effects of nervousness, with the possibilities of obsessions, phobias, and even perversions, can be something horrendous.

God gave you your feelings — all of them. You can be assured that he gave them to help you, not hurt you.

Fear and anger

Although you possess as many blends of feelings as a paint store has shades of colors, two of your most basic feelings are fear and anger.

What effect do these feelings have on your personality?

By fear we mean the uneasiness you feel when you are threatened with something unpleasant. It could be something directly painful, such as having a tooth pulled, or it could be something that deprives you of a pleasure, such as an opportunity to take a trip or receive a promotion. Your nervous system becomes tense over what is happening. If that does not work, you want to run away. If you can't do that, you might break down and cry or get angry. Your reactions will be influenced by your background.

If your fear drives you on to anger, you can act "destructively" or "constructively." You can blast your way out of the fear, or you can stand, hold your ground, and wait and see what is the best way to act in the situation.

This fear-anger reaction of your feelings is your survival kit for difficult situations. It should help you, but too often it can hurt you. This happens in the case of depression. In depression both the fear and anger have gone to an uncontrollable excess. The fear has become panic, and the anger has become rage. Your body cannot handle either for very long, so depression sets in to protect you from either or both.

Fear and panic

The serious problem that faces you is how to keep your fear from becoming panic.

You cannot eliminate all fear from your life. Nor should you try to do so. Fear is like fire. Under proper control it serves a good purpose. The problem is to keep your fear under control.

As we have seen, one answer to fear is to create a perfect image of yourself that is acceptable to everyone. Accepted by others, you not only take away the threat of harm but you also have people you can count on when you are in trouble or afraid. Unfortunately, this reliance on others to accept and help you creates fear and panic of its own.

Another answer to fear is proper medication which moderates your fear reactions. You do not react as severely to a situation as you would without the medication.

A further answer is to meet the problem head on. You ask yourself what, concerning you and your approach to a problem, is it that immediately sends you into panic?

It might take some investigating before you can answer this. A study of your background might show that your adult models reacted the same way in difficult situations. They communicated their panic to you. It might also show that you could never live up to the expectations of the important people in your life. You could not be what your parents, teachers, or clergy said you must be to succeed or to win their approval. As a result, you were constantly in a state of panic. It did not reach crisis proportions, but it was there.

Your knowing process

Besides the panic-producing problem just described, you may be suffering from an out-of-date process in your "knowledge" department that feeds your panic. This process deals with how you know things.

Children know things by "picturing" them. If they have a clear picture of something, they have an unshakable conviction about it. If someone tells it differently than they saw it or pictured it should be, that person is wrong. If children tell it differently than they picture it, they themselves are lying. It is that simple.

But what happens when life becomes more complicated and a child has to put together contradictory elements in the same picture — for example, a parent who is nice at times and mean at other times? What happens when an action has several parts to it and the child cannot see how the parts are joined together? What happens when things do not take place as the child pictures they should?

In all of these cases the child becomes unsure. If this uncertainty deals with something needed or supposedly needed, the child goes into panic.

The same is true of adults who know things only by way of pictures. If they can picture it step by step — they can handle it. If they cannot, they go into panic.

So, according to this process, the answer to insecurity and panic is to have clear pictures of what has to be done. If doubts and negative possibilities try to stampede such people into panic, they do not have to worry. They have a clear picture in their minds to refer to and thus feel reassured that everything is all right.

Disadvantages of picture knowledge

Obviously, there are some drawbacks to this picture way of knowing and acting.

For one thing, it takes a long time to get a clear picture that will exclude all doubts and negative possibilities.

For another, there is a tendency to repeat the same action over and over again until it turns out exactly the way it has been pictured in the mind.

Both of these ways of acting are nerve-racking to the person relying on this system of pictures; and they can become a source of embarrassment to everyone.

This routine can also become a source of panic to the person using it. Take the case of Daniel, for example. While he is delaying or repeating his actions, a number of important things he could be doing do not get done. On seeing how many things he has neglected, he runs scared inside.

Perhaps the most disastrous consequence of thinking by way of pictures is this delay in getting things done. Doing nothing feeds anxiety. Daniel, in this case, frets and worries, and yet his nervous energy goes for naught. He is paralyzed by his inability to move in some or any direction. He is racing his motor in neutral.

But what can he do? With this process, as with a blurred picture on a TV set, he must wait until he sees things clearly, his way. Until he does, his panic will not go away. No matter how much he is reassured that he has no reason to worry, he is not able to listen. He is more concerned with his unclear picture than with the re-assurance.

A better method

Although all human beings use the picture method — especially when they are young — to understand things, this is a restricted way of knowing. It is better to proceed from pictures to positive presumptions. This needs explaining.

A presumption is a way of knowing based on previous experiences. If you have done something a certain way for a number of times, you can presume that you acted correctly. You base your presumption on your previous experience. You do not need a clear picture of what you have done. You have a presumption.

This also applies to future actions. If a way of acting has been good enough before, you can presume it is still a good way to act. It might not be the best way, but it is a way you know and one whose outcome you can predict. This is a positive presumption about your goodness as a person and the goodness of your action.

Unfortunately, most depressed people work with negative presumptions. Below the surface, they presume that they are not good and that their actions are not good. That is one of the reasons why they need a clear picture of what they have done or are about to do. They have to "see," by way of a clear picture, that they have not been neglectful, stupid, or careless in the past; and they want to make certain they will not be so in the future. Without that clear picture, they are under the subconscious influence of their negative presumptions.

So, if depressed persons can switch their concentration from the picture method to positive presumption, they are on the road to recovery. Their feelings would be dependent on their positive presumptions. In fact, they would need clear pictures to show them how they have been inferior or guilty before they let go of their positive presumptions about themselves.

Unhealthy fear

The Gospel story about the three men and the silver pieces exemplifies this type of unhealthy fear. The first two operated from a positive presumption about their abilities and worth. The third operated from a negative presumption. Here is a paraphrase of the parable appearing in Matthew 25:14-30.

An employer was going on a journey, so he called in his foremen and gave one five thousand pieces of silver, another two, and another one — each according to his abilities. The employer left.

The man who received the five thousand traded with them and gained five more.

The man who received the two thousand did the same. He gained two more.

But the man who received the one thousand buried his in the ground and gained nothing.

After a long absence the employer came back and began settling accounts with his foremen.

The one who had received the five thousand came forward and said, "Sir, you gave me five to work with. Behold! I have earned five more."

The employer was pleased. "You did a good job. As a reward I am going to elevate your position and give you more power. Congratulations!"

The one who received the two thousand did the same and received the same enthusiastic response and proportionate reward from the employer.

But the one who buried his one thousand came forward and denounced the employer. "I know you are a stern man. You reap where you have not sowed. Being afraid of you, I buried the one thousand in the earth. Here, take what is yours."

The employer was upset with him. "You knew that I reaped where I did not sow. Why, then, did you not put my money in the bank where I could have gained interest on it? You, there, take the money from him and give it to the employee who has the ten thousand. For to everyone who has shall be given, and, from the person who does not have, even that which he seems to have shall be taken away."

Healthy fear

The above story teaches us that God expects us to act despite our fears.

So, it is not fear that makes a person depressed. The truth is that fear is natural and normal. It is an "alert" system that makes you aware of danger or evil. It helps you to cope with what is threatening you. It is advantageous and healthy to have such a system. It is unhealthy when the alarm goes off for little or no reason or it immediately pushes the panic button. That is what needs correcting.

The differences between normal fear and panic can be seen from the reaction to each.

NORMAL FEAR CAUSES ONE:	PANIC CAUSES ONE:
to be hurt and frightened by a cutting remark;	to be devastated and obsessed by it;
to be concerned about the increase of crime;	to refuse to go out or to be excessively worried while out;
to be frightened over the high cost of living;	to be consumed with worry over money matters;
to be nervous and uneasy over the death of a relative or friend;	to be paralyzed and unable to cope with the loss of a relative or friend;
to be worried and concerned about bodily sickness.	to be convinced that every illness is cancer or a deadly sickness.

This list could go on and on.

The main difference between normal fear and panic is the consuming intensity of the reaction. With normal fear you become tense and ready to act. With panic, although the body, arms, and legs might shake and are in motion, ordinarily nothing is done about the situation.

So, fear-panic plays a large part in your depression. Somehow you need a way to tone down your fears and not let them panic you.

Anger-rage

Another important factor is anger-rage.

56

As we have seen, anger is a secondary reaction to fear. The first reaction is to want to run away — from the fear or from what is causing it.

Fortunately, anger is one of your strongest weapons against a threat or danger. Properly released and used, it can protect you in the most difficult circumstances of life. Even in less difficult situations it can help you be independent and assertive.

But anger that has become rage is a very dangerous weapon, whether directed toward others or toward self. With rage seething inside of you, you are like an overheated pressure cooker. You are not sure if or when it will explode.

Rage is the product of panic. One leads to the other.

What are its causes? Rage has two sources. Either you have developed an image or social personality that does not allow you to feel anger, and so subconsciously it festers into rage; or you have been spoiled into believing that you can always have what you want, and secretly or openly you are outraged when your "rights" are violated.

Bad effects of rage

The bad effects of rage contribute to your depression in two ways.

First, if you try to handle rage by pressing down on it and not allowing yourself to feel it, that down pressure is itself a form of depression. Having a down pressure on your panic and a down pressure on your rage adds up to two down pressures and a solid depression.

A second way rage contributes to your depression is that it makes useless the anger that could help to free you from your fears.

Rage is anger gone wild. It urges you to do something, anything, rather than do nothing about your unbearable situation. In a way, that is good. At least your anger is being released. But for all practical purposes, that is bad. You do not care what you destroy or what damage you could do to yourself or to others. Actually, acting out of rage only makes matters worse. In the end, you will need to be rescued or protected. That could be scary and provoke more panic and rage.

In addition to the turmoil described above, you could turn people against you. Whatever help or understanding others might have given you is usually lost when you resort to outbursts of rage. Ordinary people in ordinary circumstances of life cannot handle such destructive outbursts.

So, anger that actualizes rage is useless in helping you to overcome your depression. It must be toned down and brought under control to serve any constructive purpose.

Two ways to correct

What can you do about anger that has led to rage?

The first thing to do is to recognize that what you are feeling is rage. So many are not aware that they are in a rage over something that has happened. "Oh," they exclaim, "I knew I was upset, but I did not realize I was in a rage. Now that you mention it, I see you are right."

The next thing to do is to try to reduce your rage. This is not easy. It is like trying to put out a forest fire. Now, try to avoid people who enrage you. If you cannot do that, you can try to approach them in a way that will not provoke them. You might not realize it, but subconsciously you could be provoking others so they will get angry at you. This will justify your getting angry at them, and then you can vent your rage without feeling you have been unfair or guilty.

Of course, if you could reduce your panic, you would also reduce your rage. We will treat this more at length in a later chapter.

Healthy anger

Of itself, anger is normal and healthy. It does not cause depression. It helps you to cope with or free yourself from the dangers that are threatening you. It is a remedy for fear.

But, as we have just considered, anger that has passed over to rage is anger gone too far. It is more of a hindrance than a help.

Here are some of the differences between normal anger and rage; they should help you see more clearly what you are experiencing.

NORMAL ANGER CAUSES ONE:	RAGE CAUSES ONE:
to want revenge against an attacker;	to want to kill an attacker;
to be upset about an attack on one's reputation;	to want to ruin the attacker's reputation, no matter how;
to be agitated and ready to quit when a job promotion goes to another;	to want to destroy the whole company for being passed over;
to be restless and unhappy when one is called on to take care of an elderly, uncooperative parent;	to slam doors and break things because one is trapped into a caring position;
to be envious of the success of others.	to want to kill oneself because of envy of others' success.

As you can see, normal anger can and should be a part of your nature at any age. It is hoped that, as you get older, you will have the prudence to know how to use it constructively. On the contrary, rage shows a lack of control. Children have tantrums; adults should know better.

Some significant insights

So, your depression is not a single down pressure. It is a number of down pressures to keep your excessive emotions in check.

There is a down pressure on your panic. There is a down pressure on your rage. There are other, lesser down pressures on your sadness, hatred, jealousy, and other negative feelings.

With all of these pressures weighing on your nervous system, is it any wonder you feel the way you do? It is amazing that you have been able to survive so much pressure. All of this down pressure and the reason for it is one insight to keep in mind.

A second insight is to realize that when you make an earnest effort to overcome your depression you will be dealing with layers of pressures.

With your hope restored, because you have read something helpful or have found someone who can be beneficial, you might feel that you have completely conquered your depression. Actually, you have made a good start. You will need to renew that hope continually as you proceed with your recovery. As you uncover buried pockets of panic or rage, you might feel that you are lost at sea. For the time, you will be; but it will pass, and you will have recovered more of yourself by facing up to the panic or rage.

Handling your emotional needs

Although we could have considered some of your other emotional needs — that people love you and that life be fair, to name but two — we have concentrated on two of the most basic ones. Your emotions require freedom *to be* and *to express* themselves at least to you. They also require some directive force that will keep them within healthy, constructive lines.

What force is best fitted to direct your emotions?

As we have seen in the last chapter, your "image" or ways of acting based solely on what will win the approval or avoid the disapproval of others is not an adequate force of itself to direct your emotions. It tends to come down too severely on your emotions, and it is one of the main reasons why your emotions have gone to excess in the negative directions of panic and rage. So, it has a place as a consultant but not as the director of your life.

The best force for handling your emotions is your real personality. That means you as a *whole* person. Acting as a whole person, you will know the best way to fit the reports of your emotions into the well-being of your whole personality. When you do what is best for you as a whole person you show that you know how to deal with your fear or anger. Your determination not to let a part of you, either your fear or anger, control you is the most powerful way to stop them from taking over or going to excess. (For more on a healthy self-control of your emotions, and your "image," read *How to Develop a Better Self-image*, by Russell M. Abata, C.SS.R., S.T.D., available from Liguori Publications.)

So, your emotions need both a freedom to make their reports and a supervisor to organize and use them constructively. If these needs are not met, you are in trouble. Your depression indicates that action is needed in this area.

Betty's middle-child syndrome

At thirty-one, Betty has backed herself into a deep depression. She is so desperate she fears she might harm herself.

Almost without realizing it, Betty shifts back and forth between panic and rage.

When she feels panic gripping her she becomes a helpless child. When she feels rage she thinks she can take on the world. She does not care about anything or anyone. She does not even care whether she lives or dies.

How did Betty get this way?

Betty is a middle child of a large family. No one ever treated her badly. They just did not have much time for her. She did not dare act up or complain to get attention, so she resigned herself to being a kind of nonperson. She had no opinions or goals of her own. She would go into a panic if she had to take the initiative in anything. She suffered from what is often called "the middle-child syndrome."

Betty lived at home until all her brothers and sisters married. She was then left alone with her parents. "Good," she thought, "at last I can get all of my parents' attention." But a cynical inner voice rebelled, "It is too late now. Besides, look at the price you will have to pay. Who do you think will have to take care of them?"

Betty felt trapped. She wanted to vent her rage toward her parents for neglecting her, but she was afraid to. If she destroyed them or turned them against her, what would she do? Not able to live with the fierce emotions inside of her, Betty became horribly depressed.

In a way, she had found the perfect imperfect answer to her panic and rage. It was perfect because being sick she could get her parents' attention and not have to make any decisions that would stir up her panic. It even gave her a chance to get back at them, because her sickness excused her from having to take care of them.

It was imperfect because depression is not a real answer. At best, it is a costly protection until a better answer can be found.

Philip's quandary

Philip is forty-seven. Married, the father of four children, he divorced at the age of thirty-two. He has had such a serious bout with depression that he has been seeing a psychologist twice a week for six years.

What made Philip realize he needed professional help?

One Monday night in a bar Philip had a disagreement over a football play with one of the barstool occupants. Philip was so enraged that he picked up his beer bottle and was about to launch it at the other person's head. Fortunately, others stopped him. He did not know how to control his temper. This had ruined his marriage, his career, and now he had made a fool of himself over a stupid football game. This convinced him that he needed help.

Philip's therapy taught him many things about himself, but the main thing he learned was how afraid he was of people. They, anyone, could upset him terribly. If someone did not agree with him and praise him for his intelligence and wit, that person had to be destroyed because he or she had killed or tried to kill something in him — his "image." It was that simple, that horrible.

Slowly, as Philip talked about his panic and rage, they began to lessen to fear and anger. Having lowered his grandiose "image" of himself, he went from being aggressive to being assertive. He learned to state or assert his feelings and opinions, and others could take them or leave them. His well-being or worth did not depend on impressing others.

In stages, Philip's depression left him. He would get down at times if people did not like him or accept him, but he could live with that and wait until his feelings worked themselves through.

Questions

1. How do you look on your feelings? Do you regret having feelings? Would it be easier to do things from routine and without feeling anything? Would that be human?

2. Are your emotions free to let you know how they are reacting to things? Or are they bottled up or buried somewhere because they are not "nice" feelings?

3. What part does fear play in your life? Do you live with fear as a constant companion? Could you be frightened and not know it until it reaches panic proportions? Is fear an unhealthy emotion?

4. How do you know things? Do you have to have a clear picture before you can act or feel safe to act? If you do, how do you handle all the negative possibilities that can come into your mind? Must you account for and eliminate every one of them before you can feel secure? Do you often repeat actions?

5. Do you presume that you are a good person and that your actions are good actions until clearly shown otherwise? Or do you presume the opposite? The man in the Gospel story who buried his money — what did he presume?

6. Do you panic easily? Over what? Does your panic come from having more demands put on you than you feel you can handle?

7. Are you on friendly terms with anger? Do you see anger as something "bad" — a sin or something not becoming a nice

person? If you are enraged, do you recognize it? Do you see rage as an anger within an anger or an accumulation of anger? Do you keep a list of all the things that go wrong over a day, a week, over a lifetime? Would it help to deal or settle with each anger situation as it happens? How does rage add to depression?

8. Are you aware of yourself as a "whole" person and not just an "image"? Have you ever used the principle: Who is going to win here, my whole self or a part of me? Who won? Are you determined to continue to use this principle until your whole self wins?

9. Can you identify with Betty and her dilemma with her parents?

10. Can you identify with Philip and his quick temper and rage?

Chapter Five
Unsatisfied Physical Needs

Having considered your social and emotional needs, we will treat in these next two chapters your physical and spiritual needs. We have followed this arrangement both because your social and emotional needs contribute so much to your depression and because your social and emotional equipment have as their main purpose to protect your physical and spiritual lives.

Living with others in society, you have the pooled resources of many heads and hands to help provide for your physical needs. Likewise, your knowledge of history, philosophy, and religion afford the necessary help for your spiritual needs. These advantages come from the outside.

Within you, your emotions or feelings are also concerned with whatever will help or hurt your physical and spiritual life. To protect you, they become intensified — even to the point of exaggeration — when either your physical or spiritual life is in danger.

Here we will consider what are your real and unreal physical needs. A good deal of your panic and rage arises from needs that are not really worth the price that must be paid.

Your basic physical needs

By your physical needs we mean all the basic material things your body requires to maintain itself in normal health.

On the positive side, this would include an adequate supply of air, food and drink, and sufficient sleep, exercise, and recreation.

On the negative side, it would exclude the extremes of heat and cold and the pain suffered from violence and disease.

To be acutely deprived of these positive elements or dangerously exposed to these negative elements could endanger your health and even your life. These are your basic physical needs.

Your physical needs are not fulfilled by an accumulation of material wealth or the possession of spectacular physical features. Wealth and physical beauty, wisely or unwisely, cater to your social needs.

Likewise, the urge to grasp every pleasure and to avoid every pain, or the desire to have something simply because others have it, are responses to your emotional, not physical, needs.

Also not included here are those things that promote physical comfort. These are all the things you need for your physical health but in a *better* than adequate amount or quality. Thus, basic food prepared in a simple way would be adequate for health. Food prepared to a gourmet's delight may be more appealing, but it is not necessary for good health.

Neither do we consider sexual fulfillment a basic physical need. (This will be discussed more thoroughly in chapter 7.)

Positive areas

The positive areas of your physical needs are well known.

On the fortunate side, these needed elements for good health are treated often in magazine articles on the effects of diet, exercise, and good air on your life. These writings serve the useful purpose of making us all aware of the importance of these elements.

On the unfortunate side, at times these books and articles tend to overstress the importance of these needs. Some writers serve as prophets of doom. Instead of relieving tension, they cause panic.

Because of this, you must use your common sense in these areas of physical health. The world of nature will not betray you. You do not have to panic over what you read, watch on TV, or hear on a talk show. If you can do something to improve your diet, the quality of air you breathe, and the amount of exercise you get, you are wise to try to do so. If you cannot, then it makes sense to disregard what you read or hear in these areas.

So, all of these elements of your physical health are important. In fact, a periodic physical checkup by your doctor could be most helpful. A hypoglycemic condition (abnormal decrease of sugar in the blood) or a run-down or ailing body could be contributing directly or indirectly to your depression.

Negative areas

There has also been a great deal written about the negative factors that can affect your physical health. Headlines glare with reports of a lack of heat in winter, the threat of disease, our endangered economy, and the rise of crime and violence everywhere. These reports sound like biblical warnings about the end of the world.

Surely, no one who understands all this can disregard these negative dangers to health. A summer/winter weather crisis, a look at how many are stricken with cancer, and exposure to violence and crime reports are enough to frighten the strongest. Add inflation, unemployment, and constant world turmoil to the list, and the wonder is whether anyone can survive. These are facts. This is reality. We live in difficult times.

Here, again, you must use your common sense to keep a proper balance. Every age has had its dangers. History testifies to that. Plagues, starvation, wars, oppression, slavery, and other calamities have always been destructive elements in our world. They are like boulders on life's road, preventing us from speeding down a smooth highway.

What can you do about these obstacles?

Much depends on you. You can consider these obstacles insurmountable and stop trying, or you can look for ways around them or over them. It is hoped that you will look for ways to cope with them. We will treat this more thoroughly in a later chapter.

The "good" life

Without minimizing any of these physical needs and without playing down the importance of suitable surroundings for human living, we want to emphasize that frequently the most pressing part of satisfying such needs is not the needs themselves but some other factor. Many times people who have real physical needs are less depressed than those who have a sufficiency or even an abundance of material wealth. Somehow, those who are deprived, if they are hopeful or are working toward a better way of life, seem to cope with life even though their physical needs are not being completely satisfied.

This is one of the many strange truths of life. It *seems* that when people had less they were less depressed.

So, in our modern times of sufficiency and abundance we have countless numbers of people who are depressed over a lack of material things when they really have enough to maintain themselves and their health.

Where does their depression come from?

Obviously, this is a complicated question and would need a considerable amount of space to reply; however, some of the answer can be found in the phrase "living the good life."

If you are seeking to live the "good" life with all its conveniences and social prestige, then you will need an abundance of material wealth. The good life and all it embraces is like a room without walls. It can never be contained, and enough is never enough. If a relative, friend, or someone else has more, you become dejected. You feel inferior. Like a child in a toy store at Christmas who is deprived of all the fine gifts that others are getting, you feel left out completely.

Personal conflict

So, a conflict arises in the lives of many — a conflict over the goals they set for themselves concerning the accumulation of material goods.

This can be a very difficult conflict for people in their forties and fifties. These are known as the "hurricane years." The heart attacks and nervous breakdowns suffered by men and women at this age are often a direct result of such conflicts.

What causes this?

Again, a simple answer is inadequate for such a complicated question. However, it would appear that the pursuing of present and future financial security for one's family can cause more stress than the human body can take. Countless days of pressure can result in an explosion within the person's physical being. Even if an explosion does not occur, a condition called "burn out" can happen. Such a pressured person is left prematurely old and worn out from all his or her physical and mental activities.

Christ referred to this total absorption with the accumulation of material goods: "What profit does he show who gains the whole world and destroys himself in the process?" (Luke 9:25) He was so aware of the anxiety and panic that comes from striving obsessively for material things that he preached against it constantly. And his warning about becoming material-minded is quite ominous: "Wherever your treasure lies, there your heart will be" (Luke 12:34). These, then, are some of the pitfalls in trying to satisfy your physical needs.

Social conflict

Besides the personal conflicts described above, there is also a social conflict arising from the anger and rage of the poor. It is the struggle between the "haves" and the "have nots."

Much of the crime on our streets is drug-related, but this violence stems from the living conditions in the homes of the poverty-stricken. The "have nots" are not content to live with their deprivations. They want to share in the wealth of the world.

"That is all right," you might say, "but why can't they work for a better life like everyone else? Why do they have to resort to violence and crime to get what they feel they are entitled to?"

That is a logical objection, but, unfortunately, people who are enraged because of their lengthy deprivation are not in a logical frame of mind. They are more in an emotional, fair/unfair frame of mind; and they do not feel it is fair for others to have more and for them to have less.

This is a problem that world leaders are seeking to solve. God intended the earth and its wealth for everyone. Obviously, material wealth is not evenly distributed. Political leaders should see to a better distribution of wealth; otherwise, they may have problems on their hands that will become too enormous for them to handle.

Sorting out your life

Are you depressed over an absence of material things? Then you should take a good look at yourself and sort out your life.

If what is depressing you is the lack of comfort derived from the "good" life, then you are not answering to basic needs but to acquired needs. You are responding either to social pressures or emotional fantasies. Neither is worth paying the price of depression.

Even if what you lack is necessary for good health, that does not have to depress you. If you are accustomed to being deprived, you might not be depressed at all with poverty, sickness, and even the dangers of death. If you are not used to being deprived and feel the pinch of need now, or foresee it in the future, then you could become very depressed.

So, although not satisfying your physical needs is one of the four causes of depression, it is not an automatic cause. Some of the poorest or sickest people are not depressed. Some of the richest and healthiest are. It seems that it is a person's attitude that makes the difference.

Your attitude

What is a healthy attitude toward your physical needs and material things?

As to what you need for your physical comfort, ordinarily it is better to have than not to have. To be deprived of physical comforts can have a negative effect on your whole personality. Of course, if you choose to deprive yourself for a worthy purpose, the deprivation can strengthen your whole personality.

As to what you need for your physical well-being, ordinarily you should make an earnest effort on your own and not wait for others to provide for you. You do not have to make extraordinary efforts, especially in the use of costly medical techniques, to prolong life.

What if — because of hard times — you cannot obtain what you need? In most advanced countries, there are provisions for people who cannot provide for themselves. They are not "great," but they are adequate. You should contact or have someone contact the agency that deals with your need. Often there is bother, red tape, and some embarrassment involved in seeking public help, but it is worth it. Besides, those filling such jobs often have a sense of dedication and understanding. They will try to help you.

You can gain a proper attitude toward your physical needs by taking to heart the Gospel phrase, " . . . blest are the poor in spirit: the reign of God is theirs" (Matthew 5:3). You will be blessed or happy when you detach yourself from material things. By detaching yourself from them, you make certain that you are not possessed by them or by anything or anyone. You are free. You accept material things, including your physical health, gratefully. You can enjoy everything, but you are not destroyed when you have to do without.

If you can acquire or work at acquiring such an attitude, you will find it easier to accept deprivations.

Connie's crisis

Connie was married and in her early fifties when she went into a deep depression. She had always been high-strung, but her ready smile and eagerness to help others covered over or mitigated the effects of her nervousness. "That's the way she is," her family and friends would say of her.

Then her father died and left the main part of his inheritance to his second wife. Connie and her sisters received only what remained of their mother's jewelry. Connie was beside herself with rage. Her stepmother would receive several hundred thousand dollars, and she would get some valueless jewelry. She turned to her sisters for some direction and support, but they did not seem to mind their father's distribution of his earthly wealth. Obsessed with the idea of her father's betrayal, she became depressed. She withdrew into herself where no one could reach her.

Was Connie's depression caused by the loss of the money? That certainly entered into it. Her husband made good money, but everything was so expensive. The extra money would have taken the edge off things and made life a little easier. But what really hurt Connie was the threat to her value system. Her father had always preached fairness, and now he had disregarded it. She could not cope with this. With so much inner hatred and rage, her depression provided a protection against such intense feelings.

Chuck's enigma

Chuck went into an acute depression at the age of fifteen.

How can a person so young and full of life and hope in the future become depressed?

At fifteen Chuck was not full of life and hope. Severely stricken with polio, he was told that his life would depend on the support system of an iron lung.

At first, Chuck did not believe the doctors, but, gradually, the truth hit home. As it did, he became terrified over his future. He could not accept what was happening. In anger, he fought with everyone — his parents, the doctors, even God. He would have no land to till, no family or children of his own, and no health he could count on. For the rest of his life, he would be dependent upon others and a machine.

Since his rage and fighting accomplished nothing and his frail body could not endure the pressures of such heavy emotions, depression set in. He had no fight left in him. Somewhere in his feelings he had died.

When Chuck was eighteen, his depression began to subside. He realized that if he were well and out of high school he would have to choose a career. He would have to do the same even if he were not healthy. What would he choose?

Chuck had to think about that. He had some help in making his choice. Periodically, he had to check into a hospital for various reasons. While he was there he observed other people who had better health and more wealth than he — even these were bitter and depressed over life. Gradually, he began to realize that maybe health and wealth were not everything. They were tools that made life easier to live; but they were not as important as life itself. He began to smile a lot, and the other patients and even the staff workers were heartened by it all. What did he have to be happy about, and if he could be happy in his condition, what were they complaining about? Strangely, seeing him smile, they went away smiling.

That, he thought, could be his career — to be grateful for what he had and to show it with a smile. He was not sure how he would do it, but he would try. The more he helped others to smile, the more his depression lifted.

Questions

1. What physical needs do you find the most difficult to satisfy? Are you always short of money, lacking in sleep, sagging from a lack of exercise or recreation? Are you always sickly? Are you upset over the increase of crime and violence in your surroundings?

2. Do sensational newspaper, magazine, or radio reports of shortages or dangers make you act more carefully or do they scare you so much that you practically retire from contact with others? What

age groups do these reports affect the most? The young, the middle aged, or the elderly?

3. What is your idea of the "good" life? How much material wealth would make you happy or happier? Would your value system make you feel better sharing in the good life or living a "good" life? Are you tired of believing that virtue is its own reward?

4. How do you feel about underprivileged groups who — during a blackout — resort to plunder? Do you feel that it is unfair for some people to have so much and for others to have so little? Do you think our leaders are that concerned with equalizing wealth? Should they be, or is it better for everyone in the long run to let the rich become richer, as long as they provide jobs and wealth for the country?

5. How do you feel about material things? Do you feel at times that they possess you? Does worry about them possess you?

6. Do you feel that Connie's feelings toward her father, step-mother, and sisters are normal? Are they healthy? What would be the best approach to such feelings? Deny them? Have them, but try not to let them get the best of you?

7. What do you think of Chuck? Does he seem too good to be real? (Actually, people like Chuck do exist.) What can you learn from Chuck?

Chapter Six
Unsatisfied Spiritual Needs

Having considered your social, emotional, and physical needs, we now treat the most important of all — your spiritual needs. Our purpose here is to help you recognize them and to point out ways of fulfilling them.

In a certain sense, it is easy to ignore your spiritual needs. Your spirit — unlike your body — does not scream out when it has been neglected; and yet it has its own ways of attracting your attention. A time will come when you ask, ''What is life all about? to be with others, to feel things, and to have a full stomach? Is that all it is? Isn't there more?''

When you ask such questions or tire of what is only material, you have become aware of your spirit's need to reach beyond the tangible to the spiritual realities of higher ways of knowing and loving. If you do not find satisfying answers when these needs reveal themselves, then your whole being is standing on shaky ground. And unless you are careful you will sink into a bottomless depression.

Your spiritual needs, then, are very important to you. In some ways they are the most important. Answering them correctly can help you compensate for other needs that cannot be answered adequately.

Your spirit

As a human being, there is a part of you called your spirit. Although it is closely connected to your body, it has a capacity for acting that is different from the way your body acts.

It has a way of knowing that is above sense knowing. This power of your spirit is called your intellect or mind. Although it uses your physical brain, it is different from your brain. With your mind, you are able to be immersed in, but not anchored to, material things. You are able to find out the secrets of nature, arrange them into sciences, and use this knowledge to your advantage. You are able to go beyond surfaces to find the underlying truths of things, actions, and people.

Your spirit also has a way of responding to knowledge that is above the reactions of your emotions or feelings. This power is called your will. With your willpower, you are able to go beyond the attractive covering of things, actions, and people to their enduring goodness. You are able to take apart the reports of your image and appetites and emotions to see what is good for you as a whole person.

So, your spiritual powers of mind and will are capable of sifting out what is truthful or real and what is good. That is when these two forces work best. They are restless until they find their rest in truth and goodness.

Your spirit's goal

Your spirit seeks to find out what or who is responsible for the truth and goodness in the things and people in the world. Of themselves, things and people are like empty containers. Who fashioned these containers and filled them with goodness? Who taught the earth to spin around the sun in such a way that it does not get too close or too far away? Who taught a seed how to grow? Who planted all the emotions in the human heart? Who has been at work in our universe?

To quiet all this questioning, we have to play detective and do some investigating. By following the clues we immediately arrive at a general answer: It must be someone with intelligence and goodness who has been at work in us and in our world.

Given this start, our minds seek to know more. Who is this someone? What is he like? Is he like us? He must be; or better, we must be like him. What can we call him? Does he have a name? We will give him the name God, so we can call out to him wherever he is. Since a name contains the whole person, this will help us talk to him and with him, person-to-person.

This simple, natural search for the reason of things and people is a solid introduction to God. As we begin to enter into a person-to-person relationship with him, we plunge into an experience that is endless in its possibilities of knowledge and love and joy. With the psalmist we can say, "You put gladness into my heart, more than when grain and wine abound" (Psalm 4:8).

Objection

"That is well and good," you might object, "for someone who has a clear head to find God or who has a living relationship with him. But I don't know where to find him. I've looked for him in vain. Besides, he can't be very interested in me. Would I be in this miserable condition if he were?"

Your objection is real. You are hurting too much and you are too tired to go anywhere in search of anyone, especially God. And if God cared — the way you need him to care — he would be there. You would not have to go looking for him. That is the unfortunate story of your life. You have always had to go looking for others to understand you and to care, to really care. You would not feel so desperate and lonely if they had.

So, what are you to do? Is there any way to break this stalemate? Who is going to make the first move — you or God?

You have to make the first move toward God. To exercise your spiritual powers, you have to tune up your mind to look beyond the surface of realities. Once you do that, you cannot help but be aware of God. He is everywhere, sustaining our creation. If he left us for a moment, we would cease to exist. It is like making an *X* by crossing the first two fingers of your hand. It takes as much for you to sustain that X as it did to make it. If you stop sustaining it, the X ceases to be.

"But," you continue, "you do not understand. I am only operating on a sense-feeling level. I have to see, touch, and feel God, or it is no good. These spiritual powers you mentioned — I don't know what you are talking about."

An answer

Perhaps an awareness of God by way of your spiritual powers of mind and will is too much for you right now. Perhaps it is not. But it could be exactly what you need. As a man said recently, "I am tired of psychology and all its digging into my past. I have so many holes in me from all the probing that I feel like Swiss cheese. I want something more."

The "more" he wanted and needed was to make progress in the use of his spiritual powers of mind and will. His therapy had cleared away enough debris and emotional blockage for him to go on to his next stage of development. He was hungering for more than sense knowledge and feeling reactions. He was in need of the more solid food of mind knowledge and will responses. He was ready to exercise his rights, duties, and privileges as a citizen of the world of the spirit. He wanted to judge himself and his actions by spiritual as well as by material standards. Still able to enjoy the sense pleasures of life, he has learned to forgo them when they detract from his new-found appreciation of the spiritual. He has now become a *whole* person.

Are you ready and able to start looking at this world with bifocal vision? to see distinctly both the material that is obvious and the spiritual that is less obvious? to start satisfying your spirit's need for knowledge of things and people beyond their surfaces and for a love that reaches out for what is solidly true and good? If you are, then you are beginning to see what Saint Paul meant when he said: " . . . Eye has not seen, ear has not heard, nor has it so much as dawned on man what God has prepared for those who love him'' (1 Corinthians 2:9).

Advantages

The advantages of being spiritually active are numerous. Some are sublime, as Saint Paul hints in the preceding quotation. Others are practical. These we will treat here.

One of the most upsetting factors of depression is the desperate feeling you have that there is nothing or no one who can stop your downward fall. No matter where your feelings try to stop for safety, that spot gives way and you continue to fall further.

Where can you turn for a net to catch you?

Keeping busy, taking medication, and finding people who care can be very helpful; but these actions might not be enough to make you feel secure. A desire, subconsciously, to return to your mother's womb where you were comfortable and safe or a longing to go further back to nonexistence, these are needless when you can actually return to the source of your being — God himself.

God is the most stable basis for building a hope. Anything or anyone less than God will not do. With God nothing is impossible. (See Luke 1:37.) If nothing is impossible for God and you are turning to God for help or encouragement, then nothing should be impossible to you. '' . . . if you had faith the size of a mustard seed, you would be able to say to this mountain, 'Move from here to there,' and it would move. Nothing would be impossible for you'' (Matthew 17:20). If you have faith — a determined belief in yourself and trust in God's help — you are capable of moving mountains. You may have to do it stone by stone, but you can do it.

In the same way, with God's help, you can work your way out of your depression.

How God works

To encourage this kind of hope in God and to avoid the pitfalls of misunderstanding and disappointment, it will be helpful to take a realistic look at how God works in our world. Obviously, we cannot completely understand his dealings with us. To do that we would have to have a capacity far superior than our human intelligence. Still, we can have an adequate understanding of the way God works in our world.

It is not enough for God to be present and sustain our world in being. We can assume that if our human parents are required to provide for our well-being, so is God. "Can a mother forget her infant, be without tenderness for the child of her womb? Even should she forget, I will never forget you" (Isaiah 49:15).

But how does God care for and weave his caring into our lives without interfering with them?

Perhaps the best way to answer this question is to look at other noninterfering relationships that are more within our powers of observation.

What is the relationship between a seed and its soil, a roof and its walls, the ocean and its shore?

Each in its proper way — the seed, roof, and ocean — do not ask more from the soil, the walls, or the shore than is needed. At times the seed will cling desperately to its soil, the roof to its walls, and the ocean to its shore. At other times, the need is not as great.

Your relationship with God

The needs of the seed, roof, and ocean are similar to your relationship with God. You will always need God. The ways you will need God depend on where you are in your development.

Your life as a *whole* human being develops in three stages — physically, emotionally, and spiritually.

Your physical development is the most automatic stage of your life. With food, rest, and shelter your body grows according to genetic factors.

Your emotional development is a more delicate process. To become aware of yourself as a feeling person, as someone different from others, takes time and experience.

Your spiritual development depends much on how you have developed emotionally. It begins when you are capable of reasoning and recognizing that your willpower is different from the urges of your physical appetites and emotional impulses. You can choose to act contrary to your appetites and impulses.

Do you need extra help from God in developing these three areas of your life?

Ordinarily, you should not. God has neatly packed into the tiny beginnings of your life all that you will need to develop as a whole human being.

Sometimes, you might need to petition God for a loan of extra help because you are at a dead end in one or all of the areas of your life. This is what has happened in your depression. Your whole being has declared bankruptcy. You do not feel you can continue your life at such a cost of pain or with such a loss of esteem and hope. It is time to scream out, "God, help me, please!"

God will help

Will God answer your cry for help?

As a good Father, he has promised to help. "If you, with all your sins, know how to give your children what is good, how much more will your heavenly Father give good things to anyone who asks him!" (Matthew 7:11) Or, as Luke puts it, "If you, with all your sins, know how to give your children good things, how much more will the heavenly Father give the Holy Spirit to those who ask him" (Luke 11:13).

But, *how* will God answer your cry for help?

As we have just seen, Matthew says God will give you "good things." Luke says God will give you the Holy Spirit. So, which is it? Will God help you directly by giving you the things you need or indirectly by giving you the Holy Spirit who will inspire, encourage, and help you to work out your depression? It depends.

If you are depressed because your exalted image has suffered a severe humiliation, the Holy Spirit might help you change to a less exalted image or help you to live with a torn or tarnished image. This is what Jesus taught: " . . . and learn from me, for I am gentle and humble of heart. Your souls will find rest . . . '' (Matthew 11:29).

If you are depressed because your emotions rush out too impulsively after everything, the Holy Spirit might teach you wisdom — the ability to stand back far enough to see things at a proper distance or in the right perspective.

If you are depressed because of an excess of panic, the Holy Spirit might point out to you that God your Father is not going to do less for you than he does for the ''lilies of the field.'' (See Matthew 6:28-31.)

Direct help from God

It makes sense that most of God's help would come indirectly by giving you a greater share of his Spirit. This would be the way of least interference.

God would be leaving you in control of the things around you, to work with them and to work on despite them. In this way, when you run into obstacles that your senses and appetites find difficult to deal with, your feelings can deepen themselves by working out the difficulties. Your spirit can do the same when your feelings run into difficulties. Besides, other Spirit-inspired people can help you work out your difficulties of body and spirit. This can strengthen your bond with others and their bond with you.

But, what if you need direct help from God? What if you need a miracle? Would God set aside the laws of nature to work a miracle for you? Yes, if it would not interfere with your development as a person.

How would you know what would or would not interfere with your development as a person?

The best way of knowing is to take a good look at your life. Is it in order? Is God the most important person in your life? Are you patient enough to give yourself and God a chance to work with what you have to see whether the adverse circumstances can be righted? In other words, do you have faith and perseverance in working things out? If you do, and if what you are asking for is good for you or a loved one as a whole person, you will receive it.

Formula for success

"But, this all seems so complicated," you say. "It is like a puzzle with too many pieces for me to deal with in my desperate, depressed state. I feel I need God's help. I don't know if I need his Spirit to help me do what has to be done to get better or if I need God to work a miracle and heal what is hurting in me and keeping me depressed. I am too confused to figure out the kind of help I need. Can't I leave that up to God?"

Yes, you can. Other people have done it — by leaving all the details to God. They have expressed their needs and shown their confidence in God with this simple formula: Your will be done, O God. This is what Christ did in the garden before facing his soul-trying experience of Good Friday. "Father, if it is your will, take this cup from me; yet not my will but yours be done" (Luke 22:42).

"If this simple formula is all that is needed in approaching God," you might be wondering, "why have you detailed so thoroughly how God works in our universe?"

Our reason is this: There is no one solution to human needs. If God does not come to your aid immediately or in the way you want, that does not mean he is not helping you. In all your actions, the basic question you should ask is this: "What is good for me as a whole person?" God's basic principle revolves around what will be best for you, or a loved one, as a whole person. Surely God knows better than you. And that is why you can leave the details up to him.

It is hoped that this will clear away some of the difficulties you might have in dealing with God and his ways of helping you.

Another objection

But you object again: "If God knows what is best for me and if he really cares about me, why do I have to ask him for help?

Somehow, that doesn't make sense. It seems too human, even childish. A child often has to ask his or her parents for help, since parents are not mind readers; but God knows our minds. Is God trying to keep us in our places by holding back on his help until we tell him how desperate we are? Is God that way? If he is, I'm disappointed in him."

No, God is not that way.

The main reason for seeking God's help is to keep some kind of contact with him. We are so material-minded: "What will we eat? What will we wear? What will give us pleasure?"

In our time of need we usually lift up our eyes or minds to God. And if God answers us immediately, what will stop us from returning to our material-minded ways? Nothing.

If we are in real contact with God, we do not have to ask for his help. We would have fewer real needs if we were, and they would be answered automatically in ways that would profit us the most.

Making personal contact

So the question is not so much how to petition God for help as how to make real contact with him.

How do you make contact with God?

To answer this, consider your contacts with others. How do you make contact with another person? Is it enough to make a contact by way of your senses? Is it enough to have another satisfy your appetites or feelings? Is it enough to know another with your mind? Are any of these contacts enough to make a person-to-person contact with another?

Any one of them would be enough if it represented your whole personality. If your eye or touch contact is a bridge where you pass over to another and the other passes over to you, then you have a person-to-person contact. The more bridges you have by way of your feelings, mind, and will, the more access you have to others.

All of these contacts would not be enough if in using them you or the other did not pass over.

Somehow, you know, you experience, when a person-to-person contact has been made. The experience convinces you. You do not have to convince yourself.

Awareness of God

The same is true of God.

Just to see, hear, touch, feel, or know of God does not of itself guarantee a person-to-person contact. And yet, if something you see, touch, feel, or think makes you solidly aware of God, you can have a personal contact. *Solidly aware,* that is the important phrase.

How can you arrive at such an awareness of God?

To be solidly aware of God, you must present enough factual details to your imagination to be able to localize or give God a place. He can be *in* your favorite church, a special scene of nature, the goodness of a loved one; or he can appear *as* an expanding circle around you. The more you imagine the circle of his presence, the more the circle expands. Regardless of how you picture him, he is present.

Once you have this awareness of his presence, you can speak with him, gaze at him, or simply be quiet with him. What happens then is too personal to really capture in words.

It can be an ecstatic experience like Saint Paul had. "I know a man in Christ who, fourteen years ago, whether he was in or outside his body I cannot say, only God can say — a man who was snatched up to the third heaven" (2 Corinthians 12:2).

Or it can be a more down-to-earth experience familiar to people who know the true meaning of love.

Regardless of whether the experience comes in technicolor or black and white, it is the most satisfying experience a person can have. It is being a part of earth and heaven at the same time.

Feelings of guilt

"But," you might ask, "what if my lack of awareness of God is because I feel guilty and am afraid of him? What do I do then?"

This is a serious problem. Some people — as we have seen — become depressed because of unsatisfied basic needs; others feel depressed because of guilt. A sense of guilt or unworthiness keeps them away from God. It keeps them spiritually deprived.

If guilt is adding to your depression, it is important that you come to terms with it. Is your guilt real or is it imposed on you by an overbearing conscience?

What is the difference?

Real guilt is present when you have defied the right order of relationships. The reality of God requires that you recognize him for the person he is — the most important person in your life. The reality of you requires that you have your various faculties under control, making them work for the good of your whole personality. The reality of others requires that they be recognized and respected as persons and not things. To defy these relationships is harmful to you and others. To knowingly and willfully cause harm to yourself or others incurs real guilt.

Guilt imposed by an overbearing conscience is present when you defy what was imposed on you by authoritarian people who wanted to make you according to their image and not according to your real personality or the image of God. Their authoritarian approach to life ignores the real order of relationships, and you feel guilty if you do not live up to that false order.

Resolving guilt

If you are experiencing real guilt because what you are doing is harmful to yourself and others, you have no choice but to change or try to change what you are doing. God will be patient with you as you learn to take baby steps away from your harmful ways.

If you are experiencing guilt imposed by authoritarian people, you have no choice but to eliminate or diminish its influence on your life. Such guilt does you no good. It does not really help others. Nor does God want it.

Jesus confronted a similar situation in his day. The leaders of the Jewish religion had imposed so many regulations on the people that religion dealt more with rules than with God. Let us listen in on a dispute between the Jewish leaders and Christ:

"Pharisees and scribes from Jerusalem approached Jesus with the question: 'Why do your disciples act contrary to the tradition of our ancestors? They do not wash their hands, for example, before eating a meal.' In reply he said to them: 'Why do you for your part act contrary to the commandment of God for the sake of your "tradition"? For instance, God has said, "Honor your father and your mother," and, "Whoever curses father or mother shall be put to death." Yet you declare, "Whoever says to his father or his mother, Any support you might have had from me is dedicated to God, need not honor his father or his mother." This means that for the sake of your tradition you have nullified God's word' " (Matthew 15:1-6).

If you question which type of guilt is yours, you would be well advised to consult someone who can *patiently* show you the difference.

The point to remember is this: Do not let guilt prevent you from getting well or from getting close to God. Resolve your guilt and get on with your relationship with God.

Importance of spiritual awareness

As you can see, your spiritual powers can reveal to you a world unknown to your senses. Animals pass by a book filled with knowledge and do not have any awareness of its valuable contents. When you operate only at the sense level, you ignore your higher powers. Your senses are doors and windows to the world around you. Your intellect sorts out and organizes the factual information your senses provide. And your will chooses what is really good for you as a whole person.

So, to be truly human, it is as important for you to live and operate in the world of thinking and willing as it is to operate in the world of sensing and feeling.

This awareness of the world of your spirit might not prevent depression, but at least it will help you to correct or satisfy those areas of your life that are giving you so much trouble. How often people say, "I *know* that it is something too small to let it upset me, but I *feel* terrible over it. It makes me so embarrassed or so afraid. It leaves me so hopeless and depressed." Such people should realize that their feelings do not represent their whole personality. Instead of getting upset, they should try to solve the difficulty or ignore it completely.

Obviously, then, it is important for you to be aware of and to satisfy your spiritual needs. It not only gives you a living contact with God; it also helps you to direct your feelings and efforts to goals that are truly good for you.

Frank's dilemma

Unmarried at thirty-six and without a job, Frank is constantly depressed. He has been so for several years. What has happened to him? He used to be such a happy-go-lucky person. Now he is always down on himself.

Basically, Frank is terrified over making decisions. He procrastinated so much on his job that his boss had to let him go. Frank now lives at home with his parents. Perfectionists, they find it difficult to understand and accept what has happened to their only child. Their sole satisfaction is that they are seeing to it that Frank gets the best help that is available. He has been going to a psychiatrist every week.

Added to his difficulty in making decisions, Frank is totally confused about God. He has been praying. His parents have been praying. He asks everyone he meets to pray for him, and yet nothing has come from all those prayers. He is too afraid to make the decision not to pray; but he has lost heart, and his prayers are more words than inner sentiments. Although he is too afraid to admit it, the little boy in him is mad at God.

What can we say about Frank's lack of success in getting God to help him?

It would appear that God does not want to "baby" Frank. He is already relying on everyone else to do everything for him. He is unwilling to take even small risks to help himself stand on his own two feet. To effectively help Frank, God would have to step in and completely reform his personality. Evidently, God sees that Frank is capable of helping himself with the aid of the psychiatrist. Indirectly, God will work behind the scenes, seeing that Frank has what he needs to overcome his depression.

Helen's predicament

Helen's depression hit a deep low when her landlord decided to cover her garden area with cement. His purpose was to keep the rain from draining into the building's basement. Helen was crushed.

What was so tragic about losing some garden space?

Ordinarily, such a loss would not be so painful, but Helen happened to be a cripple. She had been in a serious car accident and had hurt her back so badly that she would need crutches permanently. Doctors had operated on her any number of times, but the best they could do was to give her a shopping list of drugs to ease the pain. Her garden was her joy and promise of hope. When she saw a seed struggle to the surface in its determination to grow, it gave her courage to endure her sufferings. Besides, she felt very close to God in her garden.

Now they were taking this away from her. What was she to do? I told her to fight for her garden, and she promised to do so. That was several years ago.

Recently, Helen called. Her friends had convinced her to attend a healing service, and she had come away without her crutches. Resigned to living as a cripple for the rest of her life, she now found herself healed. She called her doctor to tell him to cancel an operation he had scheduled for her. The doctor humored her and told her to come in anyway. He could not believe what he saw. The X rays showed that her backbone had returned to normal.

What was there about Helen that God saw and rewarded? It was her faith. She had never blamed God for her injuries. Nor had she ever given up her independence. The equipment installed in her car, so she could operate it by hand, was proof of that. So God took the twisted shaft of her backbone and straightened it out. The miracle has not made Helen a good person. She was already that. It has only made her a more grateful person, because of the additional things she can do for herself and others.

Questions

1. What does having a spiritual faculty mean to you? Does it have you confused? How does your mind operate? What is your will searching for? How are your mind and will keys to your happiness?

2. Have your years of living and searching for satisfying goodness led you to God? Who is God, and what does he mean to you? Does the thought of God make you less hopeless?

3. Have you been having trouble connecting with God? What difficulties have you been having? Would you want God to change his prayer-answering service? What suggestions would you make to God on how to answer prayers, especially your prayers? Do you agree with the conclusion that in the long run it is better to leave the answering of prayers to God?

4. Do you ever have a person-to-person contact with God? Have you withdrawn from God because of guilt? Is your guilt real or has it been imposed by authoritarian people? How can you return to a more vital relationship with God?

5. Does the realization that you have an undying, spiritual side to you make physical death less frightening? Does the fact that you have internal powers more noble than your senses and feelings help you cope with your depression?

6. If you could have your say, how would you suggest that God should treat Frank and his depression?

7. What do you think of this true story about Helen? What do you think of Helen's simple approach to life and faith? Can you learn from her?

Section Three
Practical Aids in
Overcoming Depression

Relinquishment

If night held on to night
There would be no dawn.
If day held on to day
There would be no rest.
If time held on to time
There would be no life.
If self held on to self
There would be no love.
So, even as the gulls fly
Untouching but together
Side by side, across the
Fields of sky, let us,
Between whom the rivers
And the mountains and
Many miles come,
Hold on to neither
Night nor day nor time
Nor self, but giving all
Begin the perilous journey
To the Great Oneness where
All things belong in fullness
To each other.
If God held on to God
We would not be!

Chapter Seven
A Whole-Person Approach

Living in an age of specialists has its advantages and disadvantages.

With their freedom to concentrate all their energies on one field of activities, specialists have made many valuable contributions to a better way of living. This is on the plus side.

However, being so concerned with their particular fields, specialists have a tendency to emphasize and exaggerate the importance of their contributions. Follow this diet, take this drug, invest in this life-style, use this kind of therapy — and you will find the answer to all of your problems. But such a one-sided approach to life can be misleading and harmful. It can lead a person away from a total approach to his or her health and life. And this is more than evident when it comes to treating depression. Either this one-sided approach will not work or it creates other problems.

We have seen that persons become depressed because they are not answering one or several of their basic needs. The effects of this might not show up for awhile, but, unless these needs are successfully compensated for, such effects will emerge later.

We consider this total or whole approach to your depression so important that we will use this chapter to discuss it.

Examine your life

The natural question to ask yourself as a depressed person is, "What is lacking in my life? What need or needs am I failing to satisfy?"

The answer might be obvious. "I lost my job and I am worried over money matters. I am not qualified to do very many things. I am frightened to death over what is going to happen to me."

Or the answer might not be so obvious. "I am a good person from a good family and I have a good job, wife, and home. I work hard and take care of all my obligations. I go to church regularly and come in contact with a lot of people, especially on the job, and yet I am depressed. What is wrong with me?"

Outwardly, it does not seem that anything is wrong with this second person. But that might be the problem. If he is a surface person, he has not gone very deeply into his feelings, his relationships with others, or into a living spirituality. Any and all of these needs could be crying out for something more substantial. Their cry is depression.

It is difficult in our modern times for us to be indifferent to any of our needs. For one thing, our life situations can be so trying that we need all of our resources to survive. Also, there is not a human need that is not being investigated and brought out in the open. It is almost impossible to close our eyes and pretend that a particular need is not important. In the past, a good number of people did not realize the importance of their emotional and social needs. They knew their physical and spiritual needs were important because they dealt with life and death, but a person had to be rich or very educated to be concerned about his or her emotional and social needs. This is not the case today. Everyone is aware of his or her feelings and their influence on their health and happiness.

Importance of each need

When you satisfy each of your four basic needs or sufficiently compensate for the parts of you that are hurting, you will no longer be depressed. So all of your basic needs are important to you.

Does this mean they all have an equal importance? No. Some of your basic needs are to help other needs. Thus your emotional and spiritual needs are the heart of your happiness. Your physical and social needs are to assist them.

But whether they are more or less important, all of your basic needs should be attended to before they cry out with physical pain, emotional frustration, social loneliness, or spiritual emptiness. Response to a need is less costly and less painful than trying to satisfy a need after it has become acute. Once a need has been denied for a long time, you tend to answer more to desperation than need.

Besides, when you deprive yourself of one important need for a long time you have probably put an extra burden on the rest of you. For example, if you have ignored your spiritual needs and your spirit's assurance of a life after death, you probably have overtaxed yourself trying to safeguard your physical life. If this life is all you have, either you will overprotect it or you will be ready to toss it away when life gets too painful. In either case, you are placing an extraordinary burden on your emotions to restrain your fears, frustration, and sense of aimlessness.

So, it is unwise to seriously ignore any of your needs.

Value of compensation

"But," you might ask, "do you mean that I will have to stay depressed until I straighten out my emotions, solve my financial problems, open myself freely to others, and have a living spiritual life? Won't that take too long? Just the thought of waiting until I do all of that is depressing."

No, you do not have to wait until you have completely answered all of your basic needs to be freed of your depression. Even making an earnest effort toward satisfying a given need can lift you out of your depression. Also, you can use your strength in one area to do double duty or compensate for your weaknesses.

Notice how a woman may use her ready smile to compensate for the plainness of her features. By skillful use of hairstyle and cosmetics plus a flare for style she makes up for the flaws in her figure. And she becomes an attractive woman — not perfect — but very attractive.

In a similar way you can compensate with regard to your personal needs. Thus, if your physical health, external beauty, or material wealth do not truly satisfy your physical needs, a strong realization that you have dignity because you are a person can help make up for these deficiencies. Also, advancing beyond your physical handicaps to be a more feeling, spiritual person can be very rewarding.

Some of this compensation might be temporary, until you can actually satisfy the need that is lacking. Some might be permanent. In the words of the young lady who became blind: "At first I thought I would die. But I did not die. So I had to find a way to live, and I did. I used and appreciated everything else more to make up for what I was lacking."

So, compensation can be a very positive force in your life. It is not a gimmick or a magician's trick resorted to for the purpose of ignoring a weak area of your life by shifting your attention to an area where you are strong. That would be covering up a need, not compensating for it.

Avoiding extremes

As we indicated at the beginning of this chapter, there is a danger of looking for the answer to your depression in just one area of your life.

This is often evident in the area of wealth. In our money-mad society you are scorned if you are not advancing materially. The wealthy will say: "No wonder you are depressed, living where you do and with such an inferior life-style." And how do they advise you to overcome your depression? "Make more money."

Pleasure-seekers make the same kind of mistake. They say: "No wonder you are depressed; you are working too hard. Sure, you are responsible for the education of your children, but you need more recreation." And how do they advise you to overcome your depression? "Let down your hair, loosen up and live."

And, as we have seen, this same process takes place in the field of medicine. Scientists and specialists who want to reduce everything to chemical imbalance will approach you and your depression as if you were a test tube. "You are depressed because you are lacking in body chemicals or are chemically off-balanced." How do they advise you to overcome your depression? "Supply your body with the proper chemicals it needs."

Obviously, all of these single-minded approaches to your depression point out particular needs that require attention. There is nothing wrong with that. There is something wrong, however, when that one area is the only one heeded.

Sexuality and depression

In this "whole person" approach to your depression, how does sexuality and sexual tension fit into the picture? Can a person be depressed because he or she does not participate in fulfilling sex? Should your sexual needs be included somewhere in your four basic needs or should they be considered as a fifth basic need?

We have delayed considering sexuality for several reasons.

First, sexuality crosses over several of your basic needs. It has aspects that influence your physical, emotional, and social life.

Second, sexuality has been exploited by so many interested parties that it is difficult to separate what is fact from what is high-pressure salesmanship. If you hear something often enough and from enough different sources, you could be led into believing that what you are hearing is true.

Third, intense — rather than meaningful — sexuality is in keeping with our times. We are a society on the run. We are not always sure where we are running, but that does not seem to matter too much. It is the being in movement that is important. We become restless with what takes time, patience, or preparation. Sexuality, with its fast-acting ingredients of closeness and pleasure, is an example of our penchant for instant gratification. Like writing love letters in the sand, the effects of sexual communicating are washed away by the next wave of activities.

Because of these complications, we have found it difficult to say whether there is a connection between sexuality and depression.

To be really accurate, we would have to take into account what has just been said above. However, it seems clear enough to us that sexuality is more of an addition to the more basic areas of your life than a necessary part. It is an expression of you to another. It is not something essential to you. So, as long as you are open to sexuality and its possibilities, you are not depriving yourself of anything vital should you freely choose not to engage in sexual activities. We would have to say that, of itself, the nonuse of sex does not cause depression. (For a more adequate treatment on the part sex plays in your life consult *Sexual Morality,* by Russell M. Abata, C.SS.R., S.T.D., Liguori Publications.)

Overcoming obstacles

It is not easy to look on yourself as a whole person. There are so many obstacles to block your view.

Some of these obstacles arise from within yourself. Your senses, appetites, feelings — all these approach life differently. It is not easy for them to be aware of something attractive or repulsive and not act on it immediately. To keep them on hold while you listen as your intellect probes and your will decides is not easy.

Other obstacles arise from the kind of world in which we live. You are urged to buy this, go here, believe that, take shortcuts, and grab as much as you can — without wasting time to figure out what good it is or how good it is for you as a whole person or as a member of society.

As a result of this partial or piecemeal approach to life, it is easy to see or want to see your depression as a particular problem like a toothache. When you have a toothache you go to a dentist and he takes care of it. You had to go through the pain, work up the nerve to go to the dentist, and you had to pay him; but it is fairly well guaranteed that you will come away feeling better.

But your depression is not as simple as a toothache. It is an ache or pain telling you that something is wrong in a basic area of your life. You have to find out and work on what is wrong or lacking.

Perhaps you will need help in doing this, but your depression will not go away until you begin to handle life better as a whole person. Does that sound discouraging? Possibly, but it is also very encouraging because the end product of your efforts will not be just a cure of your depression. It will be a better, more total you.

Now, before you read the next section, reexamine the four chapters on your basic needs to see whether you can find out which need is causing your depression. It will help to have this information as you approach the changes proposed in the next chapter.

Questions

1. What are the advantages and disadvantages in a world where specialists predominate?

2. Have you been able to pick out which of your basic needs is most responsible for your depression? Is it your social need and your inability to live up to your image? (It could be since embarrassment and an overconcern for what others would think are responsible for most of our fears.)

3. What is your understanding of compensation? What is good compensation? What is bad compensation? Can you see the difference in the following examples of Nancy and Loretta?

Nancy has had MS for ten years. Physically, she is very restricted in what she can do. Mentally, socially, and spiritually, Nancy is a dynamo of activity. She is always thinking of things to do. She is never depressed and only occasionally down.

Loretta is a healthy, intelligent, attractive young woman of twenty-five. She, too, is a dynamo of activity. When she is not on the go, she is constantly on the phone with friends and family. She keeps in touch with so many lives, but she is hardly in touch with her own. She is often depressed and finds herself complaining about almost everything.

Although it is difficult to make a good judgment on the few details we have presented, what difference do you see between

Nancy and Loretta and their ways of coping with life? What can you do to catch Nancy's positive spirit and courage?

4. Do you feel that an absence of sexual activity can cause depression?

5. As a human being, are you more like a series of parts acting as they please or as a whole person?

Chapter Eight
A Challenge to Change

Up to this point we have tried to help you to understand the exact nature of your condition, whether you are down or depressed; and we have pointed out the major causes of depression. We now enter the important phase of change.

We will divide this chapter into three parts — learning to hope, changing habits, and starting to move again.

Learning to Hope

We have seen that the dividing line between being down and being depressed is hope. If you are heavily laden with difficult problems in the basic areas of your life but have hope that things are or will get better, you are only "down." If you have no hope, you are depressed.

Hope makes the difference.

Here are eight ways to help you to hope again.

(1) Understand hope's meaning

A first step away from hopelessness is to understand its meaning. Too many do not know what hope is all about and so they do not use this special power because they do not like the circumstances that bring it into existence. Running away from these circumstances, they do not wait around long enough for hope to develop and help them.

What is hope?

Hope is a positive inner force that comes alert when you are afraid or when you find yourself in dangerous circumstances. The greater the fear or danger, the greater is the hope of which you are capable. But these unlikable feelings of fear and danger make most persons run away and not even attempt to use their power of hope.

A person will say, ''I am so afraid I cannot handle a situation or danger.'' This is a negative reaction. If, however, a person reacts positively by not running away or by not becoming paralyzed with fear, he or she says, ''But I hope I can handle this situation or danger. I am determined to try. If I fail, it will not be because I did not try.''

Hope, then, is a combination of negatives and positives. If there is no fear, hope is not present. These negatives of fear and danger make the positive power of hope available to you. Think about that for a moment. It is precisely when you are afraid that you are capable of hoping.

So, the first step in the cultivation of hope is not to run away because you are afraid. Shaky and nervous as you are, you are going to try to do what you can to handle the situation. The words ''I hope I can, I hope I can'' express your determination not to be overwhelmed. They are directly opposed to the words ''I can't handle a situation. I know I can't.''

(2) Reduce your fears

The next step is not to become paralyzed by your fear.

Anxiety and panic paralyze you. They are fears beyond your control.

Anxiety is beyond your control because it is a forgotten or unknown fear. Like a slippery fish, it does not want to be caught. But your fear must be caught and seen for what it is. Once that is done it becomes more manageable.

Panic is beyond your control because it is fear gone wild. It is like a raging fire. It feeds itself on every negative scrap you have collected and stored in your memory. No sooner do you stomp out one fear but another and another and another flares up until you are exhausted and consumed. You are in panic because you cannot handle such a continuous outbreak of fears, especially when a number of them come at you at the same time. Somehow you have to slow them down to one fear at a time — with intervals between their outbreaks.

How do you slow down your fears? Here are two ways.

The first way is to eliminate the causes of your fears. (We will consider this in the second part of this chapter.)

The second way is to concentrate on performing one series of activities at a time. If you can concentrate on performing one action, even though done poorly, you are giving that action — not your fears — the center of your attention. That in itself is a control. (We will consider more of this in the third part of this chapter.)

What are the causes of your anxieties and panic?

Certain mental attitudes put you under more pressure than you can handle. The following "ways to help you to hope again" will aid you in changing these attitudes.

(3) Avoid "shoulds" and "have to's"

Among your greatest pressures are the "shoulds" and "have to's" that stand guard over your waking moments. They are automatic recordings that come from your training and are supported by your need to please others and be approved by them. They form a large part of your social needs.

As we have seen, of themselves, these recordings are not bad. Unfortunately, they can become so loud and so persistent that you hear nothing else. They command like little dictators, "Do what I say, or else." You want to listen to your feelings and your reason to see what they have to say in the matter, but all you can hear is: "Do, and do not question; otherwise you will be punished with uneasiness, rejection, and even guilt."

Needless to say, such a one-sided approach to life is an anxiety-panic trap. Automatic rules have you under the constant pressure to perform whether you are up to it or not.

What can you do about these "shoulds" and "have to's"?

The first thing you can do is to slow yourself down and listen to them. Whether you realize it or not, they direct most of your actions.

The second thing is to allow your likes and wants to voice themselves. Then try to encourage them. You might have a fight on your hands between your shoulds and your wants. For now, if you can see your way to doing it, let your wants win. Even in regards to the things that are really good for you, try more to *want* to do them than to *have* to do them. Instead of telling yourself, "I should get dressed. I have to get out of my room," it would be better to work toward, "I want to get dressed. I want to get out of my room."

(4) Cultivate particular wants

While encouraging your wants, it would be good to make them as individual and particular as you can. Try not to generalize. It will not help very much to want to feel better or be happy. These general wants are "finished" products. They do not move you to do anything to make you feel better or be happy. They presuppose a kind of magic that can get you to the tenth step of a ladder without climbing the other nine steps. What you need are specific wants. "I want *this*. I want *that*."

If these specific wants are small enough, they will not be too difficult to satisfy, and they will help build up your hope and confidence. If you can do "this" or "that," you can begin to do more difficult things. This was Christ's program for his followers. If they could handle little things, they would be able to handle bigger things. "Good man! . . . You showed yourself capable in a small matter. For that you can take over ten villages" (Luke 19:17).

"But, how do you learn to want something, anything, when you are more familiar with obligations than with desires?"

This can be a real problem. Sit down with yourself and let all the things you should do run to the front of your mind. Then, quietly, tiptoe around them and see if you can find some wants. Ask yourself, "What do I want to do right now?" Nothing might show up immediately, and that is all right. Give your wants a chance to speak up.

(5) Oppose the need to be perfect

Along with avoiding "shoulds" and "have to's," you will find it profitable to keep an eye on your *need* to do things perfectly. This need to act and be perfect is a breeding ground for anxiety and panic. It can keep you paralyzed in your room and bed for weeks and months.

A good slogan to learn and repeat to yourself is this: "If a thing is worth doing, it is worth doing poorly."

It is better to do something poorly than not to do it at all. If you wait until you feel you can do something well, you will wait a long time. Considering the state of your feelings, you will probably never feel up to it. That is bad. You need to do something to break the hold of your depression and the panic underneath. Doing can help. It takes a certain amount of concentration and effort to do anything. By making yourself concentrate and function, you begin to break the deadman's hold panic has on your inner being.

So, in your planning, think small. Try not to attempt anything big. That will scare you.

Try not to attempt to do anything perfectly. That will only give you an excuse not to do it at all.

Try not to make up for lost time. That has too much pressure attached to it. If you have learned to accept your limitations as a human being, that will make the "lost" time "found" time. In the school of living and hard knocks, you will have learned that happiness and peace belong to the heart that can accept limitations graciously. Obviously, this is not understood on Wall Street or in the marketplace, but that is unfortunate. There would be fewer physically and emotionally broken hearts if it were understood and practiced.

(6) Try to avoid "whys"

"Why" questions should be avoided at all costs. They are dangerous feed-ins for anxiety and panic. "Why am I depressed? Why is God doing this to me? Why did I have such a miserable childhood?"

These "why" questions are too difficult for you to answer now. They only make you more anxious and full of panic. It is better to avoid them. Later, when you have more information, the answer to these questions will come more easily. Some of them will answer themselves.

The most important reason for avoiding such questions is that they can be loaded with resentment. They imply that someone is to blame and can be held answerable for what has happened. Spending time blaming others or yourself could so enrage you that you could end up losing your willingness to try to help yourself. You could wait around for others to make amends and satisfy your needs, but you might have to wait a long time for that to happen. In the meantime, your hours and days will be filled with anxiety and panic, and you will lose many opportunities for growth as you strive to become an independent person.

So, instead of asking "why" questions, get yourself to ask "what," "how," "when," "where," and "which" questions. "What is wrong with me?" "How did *I* get this way?" "When did it happen?" "Where did it happen?" "Which choice will I make — to stay this way or to do something about it?"

The more of these questions you can ask, the more you will stimulate your mind to solve the problem of how you can help yourself.

(7) Use a positive approach

A tremendous help for coping with your anxiety and panic is a positive approach.

What is a positive approach to life?

It is a willingness to approach a difficult situation to see if anything can be done to solve it. You can wish that you or the difficult situation were ten thousand miles away. You may be "trembling in your boots," but you are willing to look at it and see if anything can be done about it. Should *you decide* that nothing can be done, then you can turn your back on it. Your decision, even though a negative one, is a positive action on your part. It is a positive approach to a difficult situation.

If you give up, run away, and say "No" to everything that is difficult or fearful simply because it is difficult or fearful, you are using a negative approach. This indicates an unwillingness to try. It is not a negative approach if in reality there is nothing you can do. It only becomes a negative approach when you are unwilling to try.

It is not easy to be positive in a difficult situation. It is easy to be negative. All that takes is an "I can't do it" answer for anything that is difficult.

A great part of your anxiety and panic comes from this negative approach. Listen to yourself and hear how many "I can't do it" responses come into your head. It is as if you have a machine that only produces negative responses. Try to stop yourself from giving an automatic "I can't do it" until you at least have taken a close look at your problem. If you find that your brakes are not holding you long enough to look and you are already on the run, then try to laugh at yourself and joke about what a good marathon runner you would make.

(8) Develop a sense of humor

Realistically, it would be good if you could laugh at yourself when you find yourself making a tragedy out of everything.

A very upset woman came to our counseling center and cried and cried and cried. I felt bad for her and her problems. For a number of sessions she could do nothing but cry. About midway through a session I said, "You know, what a terrible waste not to be able to put all those tears to good use. I can send you to Hollywood where I am sure they have a need for someone who could stand in when a crying scene is needed. I could be your agent and we would make a fortune. Better yet, we could pitch a tent on a busy corner here in New York City and charge 25¢ to see the crying lady.''

She looked up at me and began to smile. ''You mean I can at least be good at something?'' We both laughed. I am not sure what happened, but she did not cry anymore and she began to look at things differently.

A good laugh in a situation is often better than a pill, a drink, or something else taken or done to relax you. A laugh would be saying, ''I am taking things too seriously. I'm holding this difficult situation so close to my eyes that I cannot see anything else. Let me step back and see that it is only a part of my life.''

This ability to step back and see how silly your actions really are makes for humor. On seeing the whole picture, you recognize how foolish it is to make too much of a single incident. Actually, only a human being can step back in a given situation and see how foolish it is to become so serious about certain events in life.

Of course, this does not mean that you can laugh your way through life. Nor does it mean that what you are suffering is not painful or real. Your pain is real.

So, when you begin to experience pain, loss, fear, embarrassment, confusion, or frustration, it is not the time to laugh. It would be better to cry and release some of your pent-up tension. Nor is it good or acceptable for others to laugh at you or to try to get you to laugh before you are ready to see things differently. This would be totally insensitive, and instead of helping you it would only make matters worse.

But there comes a time when it is good to try to look away from your pain and try to see the humor contained in most human experiences. To concentrate only on the serious elements or dark side of things is to become tragic and panic-stricken. To step back a little and laugh at the light or humorous side of things is like opening up a window in a stuffy room.

As the writers of this book, we know from personal experience and from countless sessions with others that it is difficult to see anything humorous when you are down. And yet, we also know that you can learn to look for humor in things and situations. For example, two teachers once complained to each other, "Not only is Johnny the worst behaved child in school, but he has a perfect attendance record!"

Although there are still other ways to reduce your anxieties and panic and other methods to develop a healthy attitude toward life and yourself, these eight practical ways should be incorporated into your thinking. Renew now your act of hope. "I hope I can do the things I need to do to get better. I hope I can. I am determined to try."

Questions

1. You know what it means to be without hope, but what does it mean to have hope? Does it mean that you have no fears or doubts?

2. Are you a "should" or "have to" person?

3. Do you know people who are "perfectionists"? What are they like? Do you like them?

4. What is wrong with general wants? Are you able to break down your wants to realistic, smaller wants?

5. Are you a "why" person? Do you ask yourself numerous "whys" and then omit the little things you could do to help yourself?

6. Are you a positive or a negative person? Here are a few signs of each. To which group do you belong?

POSITIVE PERSONS ARE:	NEGATIVE PERSONS ARE:
those who believe they make their own luck.	those who believe they are always victims and that nothing ever works out for them.
those who close the books on past misfortunes.	those who keep records of all the bad that has happened to them.

POSITIVE PERSONS ARE:	NEGATIVE PERSONS ARE:
those who slow down until they are less tired, confused, and frustrated, and then try again.	those who tell themselves that they are too tired, confused, and frustrated to try again.
those who see another's success as a model of what they can try to accomplish.	those who are very envious of what others have and they do not have.
those who accept people at face value until they have reasons to think otherwise.	those who stay to themselves because people cannot be trusted.

7. When you laugh is it from a sense of humor or is it a nervous laugh or smile coming from embarrassment? When was the last time you had a good laugh?

8. Are you ready to make an act of hope or determination to do what you can to help yourself get over your depression?

Changing Habits

To make an act of hope when you have been so hopeless is a small miracle in itself. It is like trying to move a stalled car by pushing it. If the car doesn't budge after all your efforts, you want to give up.

What can you do to make the act of hoping easier and more durable or lasting?

The best thing to do — as we have already mentioned — is to eliminate the cause of your hopelessness, namely, the unanswered basic need that has you so upset. That is a big step away from your hopelessness. But don't be too surprised if, after a given need is answered, you are still not out of your depression. Your ways of feeling, acting, and your depression could have become such a part of you that they will not let go. They have become habits.

Examine your habits

A habit is a constant way of feeling, thinking, and acting. It is a routine way of being. Once a habit is firmly established it becomes a part of you. It seems like a part of your nature. It is a kind of second nature.

When you try to change your habitual way of being you have a battle on your hands. The troops that defend the habit are firmly entrenched. They are prepared to resist any attacks on the habit. They might retreat after an intense attack, but they are ready to return and reestablish the habit as soon as they can. This is the very nature of a habit.

Is this bad? Of itself, it is neither good nor bad. These troops that defend habits fight as hard for a helpful habit as for a harmful one. It is their nature to hold on. It is up to you to sort out which habits are worth retaining. Then you patiently withdraw the support of those habits that cost more than they are worth, and you begin to make consistent attempts to act in new and better ways.

Study your social image

In considering your social needs, we showed what an important part your image plays in your life. You have been trained to act in ways that are acceptable to others, and the net result should be beneficial to you and everyone concerned. We said that, as often as you can, it is wise to satisfy the demands of your image. If you do not, it will attack you and punish you with fear, embarrassment, feelings of rejection, and even with guilt.

Reinforced again and again over the years, your image way of acting has become a habit with you. It is second nature to you now.

What can you do if your image way of acting is too demanding, too negative, and too extensive? Other than giving in to panic, rage, and depression, how do you handle the pressure of not being what your image says you should be?

This is one of the most difficult questions that confronts you and every human being. Trying to live up to an overdemanding image is responsible for so much of your pressure. It is the support system of alcoholism. It is also responsible for most nervous breakdowns.

To help you to change in this area consider these four steps: recognize the habit for what it is; learn to oppose it; tame your rebellious feelings; and reject the habit of depression.

● Recognize the habit for what it is

The first requirement for changing a habit is to become fully aware of it.

The person you imagine you should be has a direct influence on your life. Examine this person thoroughly.

If you are tense in a situation, where is the tension coming from? If you feel uneasy in your stomach or chest areas or shaky in your legs and body, why do you feel this way? When you are faced with a task to perform or a responsibility to fulfill, do you grow tense because you feel you will not do it exactly right? Do you feel you are on stage? Are you afraid that what you have done will not be good enough?

These and so many other pressures you might be feeling come from the image you feel you have to live up to. They have been a part of you for so long that you might not even realize they were planted there by others.

What can you do about such pressures?

Once aware that you are acting in these image ways, try to slow yourself down. Your image is telling you what others feel and think you should do. What do you personally feel and think about the matter? To answer that question you will have to separate the different forces tugging at you — your image ways, your feeling ways, and the ways suggested by your reason.

Now you stand a better chance of choosing how to act. That will be your bottom-line decision. That will be the decision made by you and in line with your responsibility to yourself, God, and others.

- Learn to oppose it

If you find that your bottom-line decision goes against what your image says you must do, you will have a fight on your hands. It might be a more severe fight than you can handle or choose to handle at a particular time. In that case, even though the better part of you does not want to, you might have to do what your image said you should do. You might have to go to that wedding, do something to impress your boss, or show off your accomplishments to others.

But somewhere along the line if you want to be free and to have *your whole* personality take charge of you, you might have to oppose your image. You might have to put up with its pressure and threats of embarrassment and even guilt. Because everyone else is cheating, taking things home from work, or bad-mouthing the boss, you will feel image pressure to do the same. Who or what will win — your image or you, the whole person?

As you try to come out of your depression and get back into circulation, your image pressure could be enormous. If you can face up to it on your own, that is fine. If you need some kind of tranquilizer to calm your nerves so you can face people and do your work, that too is OK. And at night, especially when your image has a free stage to review your day and criticize you for not doing or saying the right thing, you may need something to help you sleep.

Somehow, you need to break the habit or automatic hold of your image if you are going to be free to make judgments that express and represent you, the whole person.

- Tame your rebellious feelings

Another habit that might need breaking or changing is letting your rebellious feelings of rage threaten you or others with annihilation in the face of difficulties.

Such feelings may conceal themselves until something goes wrong. Then, of a sudden, they throw you into panic and rage. "I can't have this. I can never have anything. Nothing ever works for me. I give up." Before you know it, you will find yourself punching walls, stomping the floor, or slipping away into feelings of helplessness. These are horrible actions and horrendous feelings. If you have felt them in your depression, you will know what they are.

What can you do about such feelings?

Once again, the first step is to recognize them. Perhaps, right now, they are not showing themselves; but you know they are there.

Try to avoid the disappointments that made them flare up in the past.

Try to let your fears and anger come out in more normal ways, despite what your image says. Learn to say, "I am afraid. I am angry," rather than wait until you are overpowered by such feelings.

Try to invoke the whole-person principle we have discussed. "Who is going to win here? Am I, the whole person, going to win or are my rebellious feelings going to win?"

If these feelings have become too deeply rooted or are too severe, you might need professional help and medication to help you break their hold.

● Reject the habit of depression

The last habit we want to consider here is depression itself. It can become a habit or a way of life.

It might sound cruel, or at least strange, to mention that even if you begin to feel better after a long depression, you might not want to let yourself know it. There are many reasons for this.

First, you might not feel like you used to feel, so you really cannot see or say that you are better.

Second, you might be afraid of jinxing yourself by saying that you feel better. A cynical little voice inside of you says, "Oh, yeah, just wait and see. You'll go tumbling down."

Third, you might be afraid that others will expect too much of you if you allow yourself to feel better. So far, being depressed has been a way of not having to cope. If you begin to feel better, you might have to cope, and the fear of *having to cope* can scare you right back into your depression.

There may be many misleading reasons for staying depressed or hopeless, but your well-being as a person demands that you leave your depressed state as soon as possible. You do not have to tell anyone, but it would be good to tell yourself. That can begin to release some of the positive feelings that have been held prisoners during your depression.

Words of caution

As you try here to break or change a habit, remember the rule of mutual exchange. For every part there is a counterpart. As we have seen, your very depression provided protection against panic and rage. Now, as you begin to feel better because your depression is lifting, do not be surprised if you should take a sharp turn for the worse. You do not feel depressed; you just feel terrible. What could be happening is that you are feeling some of the panic and rage from which your depression protected you. Now you must face them and deal with them.

Be concerned, but do not lose hope.

Although it may not feel like it, you are getting better.

Something inside of you knows you can cope with your panic and rage. Having partially broken the hold of your image and the destructive forces of your rebellious feelings, your panic will gradually be reduced to fear and your rage to anger.

This is already happening because you have been working on breaking your destructive habits. It will continue to happen as you move from the stage of inactivity to activity.

Questions

1. Have you ever tried to get rid of a habit — being too serious, complaining too much, smoking, drinking or eating too much, being critical of others or of yourself? Did you have to give yourself a lecture and point out all the harm that was coming from

the way you were acting? Were you ready to give up the habit because you realized it was not good for you as a whole person or did others talk you into it? Did you succeed with your first attempt? How many times did you have to try before you succeeded?

2. Have you ever tried to break the hold your image has over you? Have you been able to see your image as a set of impressions or recordings that are different from your own personality? Are most of your fears and pressures caused by the expectations of your image?

3. Do you have a lot of anger, resentment, and even rage stored up inside of you? If just one thing goes wrong, do they immediately explode?

4. Has your depression become a habit? As you break away from it are you often scared back into it because of the emerging panic or rage it was pressing down or concealing?

5. Are you determined to break this bad habit of depression?

Starting to Move Again

Since depression shuts off your feelings and since it is very difficult to do something without feelings, how are you going to get moving again? Will you have to wait until your feelings come alive before you can get yourself to do things? Or can you start to do some small things, even though they seem useless and hardly adequate to make much of a difference in your life?

We encourage you to try to do some things even though you do not have your heart in them. It is hoped that they will start you moving again, that they will help you break the hold of your depression and the panic and possible rage your depression is concealing. There is no absolute guarantee that this will work, but we trust that it will help. If nothing else, when you try to do what we suggest you will be attempting to apply some of the principles we have pointed out in the previous pages.

Do little things

Although you feel that your life is stalled on a side street of nowhere, you can get yourself moving again.

You can make your act of hope.

You can seek outside help, from God and others.

You can do some little things to help yourself.

What can you do to help yourself? This will depend on the severity of your depression and how paralyzed you are.

If you are so acutely depressed that you have been housebound or apartmentbound, can you leave the security of the house or apartment for awhile? It does not have to be for long, and it would be better if you could do it alone; otherwise, you will become overly dependent on others.

If you are not so acutely depressed and can function a little, can you do something to get yourself moving? It does not have to be much. It would be good if you could do it consistently. If you do it only when you feel like it, you will not develop confidence that you can do it.

If you can function fairly well but have no heart to do anything, can you do something, today, now? Can you start a letter that you have been wanting to write, see a friend, pay something on a bill you have been avoiding, stop drinking, or get to a doctor to check you out physically? The important thing is not so much what you do but that you do it *now*.

Think small

In attempting these little things, it is important to remember that you do not have to do them perfectly. "If something is worth doing, it is worth doing it poorly."

So, in planning what you can do, think small. Do not plan anything big. It is more beneficial to take small steps on your own than giant steps relying on others.

Try not to expect a big reward for the little ordinary things you are attempting. In the beginning, everyone will praise you for your efforts. After awhile, your efforts will be passed over unnoticed. It is difficult for nonprofessional people to sustain excitement over your small accomplishments. Most people do not realize what it is costing you to do what you are doing to help yourself. Try to perform your actions for your own benefit rather than for praise from others.

Remember to repeat your acts of hope before each action and when you are tempted to give up or to stop trying.

Try to find someone who will discuss with you your future plans and your present difficulties. The talking will boost your determination to do something. Besides, the other person might have some practical suggestions to offer.

Talk it over with God. Just because you are angry at God for his seeming lack of attention to you does not mean you cannot talk to him. If he seems too far away to witness your pain, shout out to him until you are sure he hears you.

Important questions

As you read this, are thoughts of little things you can do suggesting themselves?

Are they practical thoughts?

Can the action be done now?

Can you do it by yourself?

Can you put up with the cynical reaction inside of your head that seems to be asking, ''What good is this going to do when you have so much that has to be done?''

Can you really *want* to do it, instead of thinking you *have* to do it?

Can you stop comparing what you can do with what others can do? (You are you, not someone else.)

Can you try to accept the fact that sometimes what you choose to do will not turn out right the first, second, or even the tenth time?

Can you put this book down right at this moment?

Are you becoming frightened because what is written here is too ''pushy''?

Can you make an act of hope and try to act despite this fear you are feeling?

How experts can help

In this chapter we have emphasized what you, the depressed person, can do to help yourself. We have done this because what you can do to help yourself is what will make you well. The part that others play in helping you is very important. The part that you play is absolutely essential.

Here we will spell out what experts can do to help you to help yourself.

Because this consideration is loaded with dangers, we will go slowly and carefully.

If you are like most people, what you will do to help yourself get over your depression will depend on the kind of support you receive from others.

If you are dealing with a depression that is protecting you from excessive panic and rage, you will probably need competent professional help to assist you to release and deal with these excessive emotions. This release is to be done slowly. The accumulation of your rage and panic is like a floating iceberg. The top is above water. The rest is below water. Dissolve or take care of what is on the surface and more will surface, until it all disappears.

Although this procedure takes time, it is a very natural approach. Nature has a delicate awareness of how much you can handle at a given time. Experts know how to encourage this natural process of panic-rage release without being too aggressive or too passive. They know that rage must give way to explosive and aggressive anger, and that in turn to an assertive personality who is capable of expressing his or her position without demanding that others accept it.

Once you are willing to explore such confused areas of your personality, you will want an experienced, sensitive guide. You will prefer someone you can trust.

How others can help

Others who are not experts can help or give support in a variety of ways. They can take care of what needs immediate attention, like handling finances, helping others to understand what you are going through, being there when they can, etc.

Depression is a difficult time for everyone — for you the depressed person and for those who want to help.

Since this is so, everyone can use some guidelines.

Those who want to help should not discourage or interfere with your efforts to do something. They probably could do what you are doing better or faster, but that is not the point. What is important is that you do it your way. In most cases it will probably be better if others do not *encourage* you to do anything. Such encouragement will be taken as a "should" or "have to." It is up to you to help yourself on your own.

It is vitally important for your well-being and that of your helpers that they make it clear to you and to themselves how much they intend to help. You cannot define this. Only the helpers can. If the helpers do not clarify this, at least to themselves, everything gets fuzzy and the help that is given only provokes resentment because more was expected. So the helpers must be on their guard not to overextend themselves and take out their frustration on you. It would be better to do less, willingly, than try or pretend to do everything, miserably.

How to help yourself

Since your depression is a habit inside of you, only you can break it. Others can only do so much to help you. Perhaps you can only do so much to help yourself. If both you and others do what can be done, you will begin slowly to make your way out of the deep pit of your depression. But, as you expose your panic and rage, do not be surprised if you slip and fall part way back into the pit because the supports you are relying on are not strong enough to hold you up.

It is when this happens and you are tempted to give up that a friendly, extended hand means so much. This gives you a chance to hold on until you catch yourself and break your fall. With this rest you can get up and go on to face the monsters you are exposing. Obviously, this is not the time to ask a multitude of "why" questions or to blame others for your predicament.

These slips and falls are natural as you try to overcome your depression. It does not mean that God has abandoned you or that others are not helping you enough. Nor does it imply that you have neglected to help yourself in the best way possible. It is precisely at such difficult times that you are given the opportunity to develop the muscles of your hope. "I hope I can pick myself up and go on. I will try." The old expression "God helps those who help themselves" is very true here.

God bless you in your efforts to help yourself!

Jenny's problem

Jenny is forty years old and divorced. She is attractive and has a good job with a fashion firm. Lately, she has been so depressed that she has had to take a leave of absence from her job.

What brought on her depression? Was it her divorce, a promotion she failed to justify, a leg injury that had slowed her down, or the death of a friend?

Whatever it was, Jenny was withdrawing more and more from normal life. She slept late, ate too much, did not clean her apartment, and watched TV most of her waking hours.

Her older sister Susan did not like what was happening to Jenny, so she took a day off from work to clean the apartment and talk with her. "Jenny, I'm not going to pass judgment on you or preach to you. I'm worried over what I see happening to you. I do not know what to do for you, but I am sure someone does. You need help."

Feeling a little better because she had someone who cared about her, Jenny let her sister arrange an appointment with a psychologist on the very next night. Susan volunteered to go with her.

Many weeks and many sessions later, Jenny did not feel any better. Reluctantly, she went for her next session.

"Jenny, what can you do to begin to help yourself?" he asked.

"Nothing," Jenny answered.

"But there must be some little thing you can do to begin to build up your confidence in yourself."

Jenny would not promise anything, but she said that maybe she could get up by nine o'clock every morning.

"Good," the psychologist answered. "Work on that until you can do it."

Jenny did work on it and surprised herself that she could do it. She then attempted to do little things with the extra time she had. She surprised herself again at what she could do. And she was astounded at how much better she felt doing things rather than doing nothing. Although she did not know how long and rough the road ahead might be, for the first time in months she had hope that she could make it.

Questions

(These questions are meant to help you accept the challenge of change suggested in this chapter. Answers should be written out on paper.)

1. Who am I?

You might ask, "How do I answer such a question?"

The easiest way is to write the phrase, "I am usually . . . angry, frightened, whatever." Think about those whatevers until you can write a detailed picture of yourself. What characteristics about yourself have you discovered? Are they mostly negative or positive?

2. Who do I have to be?

The easiest way to answer this is to write the phrase, "I should be or I am supposed to be . . . good, smart, whatever." Again, think about those whatevers until you can write a detailed picture, an image, of the person you feel you should be according to your training, the example of your heroes, and the acceptance of your peer groups past and present. Chances are, if you add enough adjectives to the starting phrase, "I should be . . . ," you will discover the origin of most negative traits found in your first answer.

3. Who do I want to be?

The easiest way to answer this is to start with the phrase, "I want to be . . . ." Fill in the adjectives, but remember to stay particular and not just general.

It is these "want to be" answers that will motivate you the most to accept the challenges of change we have indicated in this chapter.

Chapter Nine
A Cry for Love

Although there are many ways of viewing a reality, the way that sees it with all its parts — separated or joined together — is best.

This is true with the reality of your depression. We have taken your life apart, piece by piece, and we have urged you to look for defective parts that would explain and help you correct the horrible way you feel. It has probably been hard for you to hold on to so many things at one time.

In this chapter we will try to provide a storehouse for all the things you have discovered about your depression. We will look at your depression from the viewpoint of love — its presence or its absence.

Christ neatly summed up all human conduct and happiness in terms of love. " 'You shall love the Lord your God with your whole heart, with your whole soul, and with all your mind.' This is the greatest and first commandment. The second is like it: 'You shall love your neighbor as yourself.' On these two commandments the whole law is based, and the prophets as well'' (Matthew 22:37-40).

We will see in this chapter that your depression is a cry for love. Following the order used for your basic needs, we will consider your love for others, for yourself, and for God.

Importance of Being Loved
and of Loving Others

Although one factor of our development as persons urges us to become independent of others, another factor insists that we share ourselves with others. Many parts of our personalities are left undeveloped if we do not.

Another way of stating this is that we should outgrow our *need* for others, but we cannot find a substitute for *wanting* others.

The difficulty with most depressed people is that when they depend on others to help them or approve of them, those people are not always around to help, or the depressed person fears that those people would not approve of what he or she has done.

Depressed persons do not *feel* loved. Nor do they feel that they are loving.

Do you feel loved?

There are many reasons why depressed persons feel that they are not loved. No one can understand how bad they feel. It seems no one is around when they really need help. No one seems to care. These are some of the surface reasons. The real reasons run deeper. Depressed persons are confused about what being loved means and the effects that love produces.

If they had a happy childhood, then being loved should produce the same happiness they had as children. They should feel warm because they are wanted and because they are secure from danger or pain.

If they did not have a happy childhood, then being loved should produce all the happiness they did not have as children. And this should produce a Camelot world where everything is just right.

Obviously, depressed persons do not feel either the effects of a truly happy childhood or of a fantasized happy childhood. So they do not feel loved. Instead they feel alone, hurting, cold, panicky, and rebellious. They feel cheated. If they do everything others taught them, including religious teachings, they feel even more cheated. They cannot trust anyone, especially those who say they love them. Life is a game, and they always seem to be the losers. So why try, they say, when there is nothing to hold onto — not even the will to live?

This, in varying degrees, is the kind of confusion you suffer when you feel you are not loved. If you try to feel good again by overdrinking or overusing medication to free you from your pressures, you do not help matters. You only make them worse. If you pretend you do not care whether you are loved or not, that lie wears thin after awhile or it sends you into isolation or the place called "nowhere" in your feelings.

How to feel loved

The experiences of being loved as a child are the foundations for later experiences. But you are not a child anymore.

As an adult, being loved has many new dimensions to it. Not being a child, you do not need the things a child needs — protection, constant encouragement, someone to care before you can care, etc. You might feel a need for all of these supports, but such feelings are more an insatiable hunger than a real need. If such feelings prevail and then panic you into believing they must be satisfied before you can do anything, they can stop you dead in your tracks. They can make you wait until others accommodate you in all the details of your life, like a baby.

But, as we considered in the last chapter, you do not have to take such helpless feelings too seriously. You might not be able to do everything to take care of yourself, but you can do something to get moving again. You are not as helpless as you feel.

Being loved as a grown person is having someone attracted to you because you have appealing qualities — whether physical, emotional, or spiritual. The person (or persons) who esteems these qualities in you wants to become one with you.

So, being loved means that others recognize something appealing in you. Surely there is something in you that can attract others toward you. God does not make junk. The truth is God made you rather special. It is up to you to feature the good points that will attract another or others to you. You are capable of being loved or of attracting others. Those you attract might not be externally the greatest, but they are persons in their own right. They can grow to match the goodness in you that attracts them to you.

Learning to love others

Since depressed persons do not feel loved — as they were really loved or fantasized that they should have been loved as children — they find it difficult to give love. It is not easy for them to answer these and other questions:

Will they give love as a real or fantasized parent and thus need the other person to be a child or dependent?

How will they overcome their deep resentments and secret rebellion if they felt they had not been loved?

How will they convince others that the love they are giving is real and lasting when they are not convinced themselves?

Because of these difficulties, most of the love depressed persons extend to others takes the form of service. Their love has been the gift of things, actions, and physical presence. It has not been a gift of the heart because they have yet to learn what that is.

They have to learn that giving from the heart has limits and no limits. The limits come from their capacity as human beings and the other person's ability to receive.

They need to understand that gifts of the heart arise from the authentic person, not from the inauthentic one.

They have to recognize the fact that some persons are unable to appreciate what they are giving. Someday those other persons may learn to appreciate gifts of the heart. Until then, it is foolish to place the blame on themselves or the gifts they have given.

Instead of blaming themselves, it would be better if they faced the challenge head on. This is a matter of "wanting to." They must want to learn what will expand their hearts so that they can lift themselves off the ground and away from their depression.

Ways to practice love

Where or how can you learn to accept another's love and give your own?

There are a good number of courses given on love. Some are good and some are not so good.

There is the course your parents gave you. They taught by word and example. You had to attend their school.

There is the course that religion gave to you. It was taught by preaching which emphasized rewards and punishments. You probably had to attend some of its classes.

There is the course depicted in books and magazines and derived from movies, television, and street talk. You probably picked up more from these sources than you realize.

Then there is the course of personal, practical experience. Rightly or wrongly, it has strongly colored your ideas of love. Most likely, it has made you question whether such a reality exists, or, if it does, whether it is really worth wanting.

Love is a reality. It is the fourth dimension of reality. All the reality we know has come from a loving mind and loving hand — God. All reality functions best when it is fired by love.

Love is possible, available, and can be yours to receive and to give; but you must work at it. You are not a baby anymore. As with any other lofty, human experience, you would do well to stop and examine yourself in terms of love. Do not generalize that you do not know anything or that you know everything about love. The truth is probably somewhere in between.

So, practice receiving and giving love. And be practical. Do not shoot for the stars or even the moon. Keep your sights here on earth. There are plenty of people on whom you can practice. Start, and even stay, with little acts of love. Be grateful when you receive them and joyful when you give them. By constant practice you will eventually produce something worthwhile.

Importance of Loving Yourself

As we have just seen, your depression derives from others not loving you or you not loving others; but its ultimate source is a lack of love for self.

Christ said, ''Love your neighbor *as* yourself.'' In other words, ''put your neighbor in the place of yourself and love him or her as you love yourself.'' Unfortunately, because you are so often down on yourself, following Christ's rule would not put your neighbor in a very enviable position.

What Christ means, and what happiness demands, is that you *really* love yourself. True self-love insists that your image or the person you have been trained to become should take a backseat when it imposes too many negatives. It also summons you to slow down your impulsive emotions and sort them out, to see whether what they want is really good for you as a *whole* person.

How to love yourself

To love yourself takes work. To use the tactics described above is not easy. But the most difficult part is to carry out what you have decided, no matter how much the losing side kicks and screams. There will be times when you fail, but you must try again. Eventually, you will be able to decide and do what is best for you.

As the union of persons can be described as real love, so the union of a person's parts into a whole personality can be described as real self-love. It puts you in a position to be able to accept another's gift of self and to share yourself with another or others.

(Should you desire more information on this topic of real self-love, read *How to Develop a Better Self-image,* by Russell M. Abata, C.SS.R., S.T.D., order from Liguori Publications.)

Importance of Being Loved by God and Loving Him in Return

When a man and woman unite in true love each one crosses over the line of self to the other. Like magnets to steel, they are attracted to each other. Each desires to be with the other constantly. Neither wants to leave the other. But when they must part he takes with him something of her and she takes with her something of him. They both revel in their past experience of mutual love and anticipate more of the same in the future.

God loves you

When we apply this knowledge of love to God, we ask, "What is there in us that could attract God to us? What do we have that could make him go out of himself and want to be united with us? Compared to him, we are nothing. What attracts him so?"

To *really* understand the power we have to attract God would require more intelligence than we possess. At best, we can only discover and accept the fact that God finds us attractive. We are fortunate that it is so.

But, even though our intelligence cannot completely penetrate so deep a mystery, we can try to understand some of it. An artist who paints a masterpiece will stand back to admire it. And if the painting begins to teem with life — actually begins to stir — he is even more delighted and attracted to what he has created.

It is somewhat this way with God. He is delightfully drawn to his creation, and more especially to us. Is it possible that the words of the first chapters of the Bible, "It is not good for man to be alone," are a projection on God's part? In speaking about and understanding Adam's desire for another human, is it possible that God was hinting about his desire to have others to love?

Aside from such lofty speculations about God and his creating ways, we know God is drawn to us. We know that what God has created is of interest to him.

How do you know?

How do you know that you are attractive to God? Do you know it only in your mind? Do you know it only by some kind of faith that depends on your moods? Do you know it in your feelings?

In the long run, it is what you know in your deepest feelings that really counts. Being deep, such feelings are an anchor for more surface, impulsive feelings. Being basic, such feelings are a landing field for the lofty flights of your mind.

How do you get such deep feelings that you are highly attractive to God?

The best way to arrive at such feelings is by experience. What others tell you and what your reason arrives at are not as convincing as your own awareness arrived at by repeated, solid experiences.

How do you become aware?

You become aware of your attractiveness in three different ways:

First, you need to slow down and become acquainted with yourself. If you continue to race through the experiences of life, you will never get to know yourself. By slowing yourself down and experiencing yourself on the many levels of your being you will find yourself a very remarkable person. Who, in all creation, is your equal?

Second, reflect a little on your attractiveness. Of all the possible people God could have created, he created you. There is something in you that caught his mind's eye. That something has to be extremely attractive to catch, hold, and convert God's attention to creative intention.

Third, look at all that God has done for you in this life and promises to do in your afterlife. That should more than convince you that God finds you attractive enough to be loved.

You know, you are a very special person. What you are capable of being — once you work through your depression and remove the obstacles blocking the full bloom of your personality — is breathtaking. You need not wonder what God sees in you.

Wanting to love

Love is like a baseball game of pitch and catch. To be always on the receiving end would require an endless supply of baseballs on the part of the one pitching. But by returning each ball that has been pitched, you pay more attention to what is pitched, how it is pitched, and the one pitching.

Mature love does not want to be always on the catching or receiving end. It wants to return or match what was received. Mature love — between human beings — thrives best where there is an equality between the persons.

And although there is no natural equality between an infinite God and a finite "you," God has bridged the gap by his grace. Because of this freely given gift, you can now love God in return. This is why your love for him should be not a matter of obligation but of privilege. You should "want" to love him because he has graced you with his love.

"But what can I give to God who has all things?"

Don't forget that God does not want anything impressive from you. He wants what you want to give him and are able to give him — no matter how small. One of the most thought-provoking scenes of the Gospels deals with a woman who was praised for giving so little. That little came from what she really could not spare. Those who had given a great deal from their abundance did not please Christ a small fraction as much as the poor woman. "He called his disciples over and told them: 'I want you to observe that this poor widow contributed more than all the others who donated to the treasury. They gave from their surplus wealth, but she gave from her want, all that she had to live on' " (Mark 12:43-44).

What can you give God right now? You can give him your determination to try to get over your depression. "But that is so little. I am not even sure I am determined to do anything to help myself." As we just considered with the poor woman, it does not matter how much you are able to give. Give what you can and that will be pleasing and acceptable.

Of course, the most important gift is the gift of yourself.

How do you love God?

One of the most precious gifts you can give or receive in your relationships is a person-to-person contact with the other. This may take time and effort, but it is what love is all about — one person uniting with another. When you unite with another by way of your sense of touch, sight, or sound or by a mutual satisfying of your appetites or by your feelings, minds, and wills you bring your individual personalities into focus. If this does not happen, then any partial uniting can be good and satisfying for a time, but it will never quite make it to the depth of mature love.

Now this person-to-person union with God is the goal of your love and your life, present and eternal.

How does this person-to-person contact between you and God come about? Prayer is the best-known contact-maker available to you. Prayer is something a child can learn and practice with the same efficiency as a scholar or a saint. It is not something that requires a great deal of knowledge or a long list of memorized formulas. These formulas have their place — like reciting or reading someone else's poetry to a loved one — but the most important factor of prayer is to become vividly aware of each other as persons and as loving persons.

Objection

Perhaps you are shaking your head and saying to yourself, "Forget it. I'm so depressed that I am not really interested enough in anything or anyone to make the effort to be aware of God as a person, a loving person. Find some other way, or count me out."

But you can be aware of God as a person. If nothing else, you can talk your situation over with him. Slow yourself down and focus your thoughts on God and away from yourself. If it has been a long time since you have really talked *with* God, begin by reintroducing yourself to him.

Try to put away your prejudices about God and how you may have been frightened of him as a child. Talk to him as you would to a friend.

"But, when I slow down, become silent, and try to pray or say something to God, I feel that I am in an empty room. No one is there. I do not feel that even I am there. What do I do then? Do I keep talking when I feel disconnected from God?''

No, you do not have to keep talking if that does not seem to be making contact with God. Stay in the silence of your mind and wait for the well of God deep inside of you to surface its living waters. Just do not give up.

While you are listening to the voices of silence, from time to time, make acts of faith in God and acts of hope in yourself and your efforts to overcome your depression. It takes stick-to-itiveness to break out of yourself and into the presence of God. By praying this way and applying to your life the helpful hints of this book you will succeed. You will overcome your depression, and, best of all, you will have discovered love, especially the love of God.

Sean's fears

The oldest of five children, Sean is a good-looking man of forty-one. Both of his parents were from Ireland and had come to New York City as young adults. They had met at an Irish dance and two years later were married.

Sean is an outgoing, likable person. He would do anything for anyone. He has a good job with a big department store and hardly ever misses a day of work. He would feel guilty if he did. That is how responsible he is. And yet, as likable and responsible as he is, Sean never married. He never wanted anyone to see and experience him that intimately. He was afraid of what others would think of him if they saw him as he saw himself.

What can we say of Sean's love life?

As friendly and outgoing as Sean seems, he has never crossed over into another's inner being or allowed anyone to cross over into his. He needs the self-esteem of having others like him, but at a distance. It is not that he puts up a wall to keep others out. He just runs away before they can get too close. He is everyone's and no one's friend.

As for loving himself, Sean is too much taken up with performing and pleasing others to slow down to see what he is doing to himself. Behind his smile, Sean is a collection of fears. Fear is the only thing that unites him. He is one fear from head to toes.

As for his love of God — being loved and loving — Sean observes the rules and rituals of religion perfectly, but his observance is devoid of life. Religion is more a burden than a blessing.

It is no wonder, then, that Sean is finding it harder and harder to smile. It is not surprising, either, that he is sneaking drinks regularly at home, on the job, and with anyone he can.

What is the diagnosis for Sean's condition? He needs love. He must learn to give and receive it.

Hilda's story

The second youngest of four children, Hilda was seven when her father was killed in a car accident. She was too young to really understand what was happening and too old to pretend that nothing was happening. Somehow she and the family survived. No doubt much of this was due to her mother's sensitive handling of the tragedy. Her mother cried, and cried openly, until she cried out her pain. Then she stopped crying and went on with living.

Hilda did well in school and was liked by her classmates. She was somewhat shy, but she had enough spunk to go after what she wanted, even if that would not seem like a whole lot in someone else's eyes. Her accomplishments included completing college, marrying, and having four children of her own.

Then lightning struck again. Her husband John was killed in a car accident. She did not know what to do. She tried to follow her mother's example of crying it out, but the tears would not come. Instead, she became severely depressed. This second untimely death opened up sealed trapdoors in her personality, and all she could feel was the sensation of falling, falling, falling. She did not know what to do.

Fortunately for Hilda, one of her parish priests was a counselor and was able to give her the support she needed to work out both tragedies. The results were that she was able to work through some of her shyness and fear of people and their power to destroy by criticizing. She also was able to strengthen the weak structures in her own personality. That was the frightening part. Eventually, she came to see the wisdom of God in her painful circumstances, and she began to work out the hidden fears and angers within her.

Although Hilda's story is by no means completed, it is a love story. She is learning and accepting that love is not always having what you want; rather it is wanting what you have.

Questions

1. Has it ever occurred to you that your depression was a silent shout for love? What does being loved mean to you? What does loving mean to you?

2. Where have you learned the most about love? Who or what has influenced your ideas of love? Do you feel that books of religion and romance — in their own ways — speak of a love beyond the reach of most people?

3. Do you love yourself? How much? Is it wrong or selfish to love yourself?

4. Do you feel that God loves you? What are the most lovable traits he sees in you?

5. Do you love God? Is it because you should or because you want to or for both reasons? How does prayer help you to make a person-to-person contact with God? Do you like to pray? Do you hate to pray? Do you pray often? Often enough?

6. What do you think of Sean and his love life? What would you tell him if you could speak to him?

7. Do you like Hilda? Do you know someone like her? Are you like her? Would you want to be like her? Could you have turned her tragedy into profit? Do you have what you want? Do you want what you have?

8. Depressed or not, can you do some practical things to improve your love life?

Chapter Ten
A Confident Look at Tomorrow

This book has been an attempt on our part to examine the roots of your sad yesterdays and to replace them with a confident look at tomorrow. We have tried to understand and to treat your depression. Page by page we have seen your depression as a costly defense against feelings that are too much for you to handle.

We have discussed your feelings of panic. Because your fear is lightning fast in detecting all the threatening possibilities of a situation, you go immediately from fear to panic. You do not know normal or healthy fear. You only know terror and horror. It seems you must be freed from all fear or you cannot live.

We have also seen that your fear-panic generates the explosive elements of anger-rage. As your fear goes immediately into panic, your anger tends to go immediately into rage. Because you cannot endure these intense feelings very long, depression sets in so you will not feel very much of anything.

What corrective feelings has nature given you to lift the lid of your depression? You have the feelings of hope. As soon as you can make a convincing act of hope, some of your depression lifts. If you can make continuous acts of hope, based on taking care of your basic needs, your depression goes away. You can still get down, but you do not become depressed.

Who will manage your feelings?

So, releasing your feelings and getting them to work for you and not against you is the answer to depression. But to get the most out of your feelings, they need a good manager.

Who or what can manage your feelings best?

It should be something over and above the feelings themselves. They do not do very well when their reports are not monitored properly.

Actually, the choice of managers — as we have seen — lies between your training and your *whole* personality.

Now the dos and don'ts of your training may give you satisfactory advice, but they must not become the manager of your feelings. It is good to know what others feel and think you should be, and it is great to be able to present a good image to everyone all the time, but it is not always realistic. For example, according to the image your training wants you to be, you should never have "improper" feelings. But in reality, you often have "improper" feelings of hatred, jealousy, anger, etc.

Is it better to suppress your feelings or to feel and deal with them according to what is good for you as a whole person?

There should be no doubt in your mind that the second approach is healthier and better.

So, the best manager of your feelings is your whole self. You feel fear, anger, panic, and rage; but you are not fear, anger, panic, or rage. They are parts of you. They are not you. It is up to you, the whole you, to manage or deal with them in the best way possible.

Objection answered

"But, this approach to feelings is so different from what we were taught," you might object. "It does not seem right to feel hatred toward anyone. Isn't hatred one of the capital sins?"

This approach might seem different from your training where feelings were looked on as a proximate occasion of sin. The idea of those who trained you was that if they could stop persons from feeling anything that could lead to sin, they would stop them from sinning.

Obviously, the idea behind this was not bad. Who wants others to sin and hurt themselves in their love relationships? No one.

The main difficulty with this approach of looking on some of your feelings as sinful is that it makes God look bad. He created your feelings.

Another difficulty is that it is not true. A sin is an act of the will. It is not a feeling. Feelings are only reports of what is happening around you and your reaction to what is happening. Sin enters the picture only when you knowingly and willingly consent to an evil thought, word, action, or omission. Evil feelings may tempt you to sin, but they are not sins in themselves.

A further difficulty is that it deprives you of a great deal of available power that you might need. To turn off parts of you is to leave you partly dead. That is not very healthy in an age as challenging as ours, where we need to know we have the power to counteract the dangers around us. Otherwise we might let evil triumph and give in to despair and helplessness.

Perhaps your difficulty with this approach to your feelings is similar to the difficulty that Christ encountered when he tried to change the thinking of the leaders of his times. He realized that his teaching about the Law and its current interpretation would sound offensive to many. His answer to this difficulty was the following: " . . . no one pours new wine into old wineskins. Should he do so, the new wine will burst the old skins, the wine will spill out, and the skins will be lost. New wine should be poured into fresh skins. No one, after drinking old wine, wants new. He says, 'I find the old wine better' " (Luke 5:37-39).

So the best way to deal with your feelings is to recognize them as feelings. They are not you. They are reporters. It is up to you to decide on the basis of your whole personality what to do with their reports. When you handle your feelings of depression in this way you can survive today and anticipate tomorrow in all confidence.

Conclusion

As we bring this book to a close, you might be wondering about the practical value of having journeyed through these pages.

Yes, you know more than you did before.

Yes, you can see areas where you can help yourself. You can also see areas where you cannot help yourself and, therefore, will need outside assistance.

Yes, you will need to read sections of this book over several times before it will produce fruit.

"Yes, yes, yes; but I can't see myself getting over my depression. It is too complicated and has been with me too long. I need someone — God, science, hypnotism — to do it for me. I just can't see my way."

It is hoped that you really do not feel this way; but if you do, then maybe, just maybe, it is not so much that you can't help yourself but that, secretly, you do not want to or won't try to help yourself. It is too hard. You have suffered too much. You are too afraid.

From the very beginning of this book we have assumed that you could not help yourself. "I can't." If you find that you are dealing more with I do not want to — I won't — then the first challenge that faces you is to change from "won't" to "will." "I will try."

Once you can say that, then reread these pages to find there the assistance you need to help yourself.

Your depression is the result of a number of twisted feelings — panic, sadness, guilt, and rage. It is worth whatever efforts it will cost you to unravel these feelings. Not only will you lessen your pain; you will increase your capacity for love. To really experience love is to really experience yourself, others, and God. There can be no greater experience than that.

Celebration: The Blessing of Self

I'm tired. The holiday celebration is ended.
The food was cooked, shared and eaten hours ago.
My preparations are memory.

I was lost today
In all the getting and spending
Of self
And I wondered
Comparing myself to the other guests
Who had done so much
And gone so much further in life
If I might ever measure up.
(I was lost so often following
Down the pathways
Of *their* experiences.)

But a peace was waiting
When I got back home
Like the indwelling of the Lord
In blessing. No longer
Fearing comparisons, I felt one
Within myself and realized
That my measuring was false;
Probably always had been.

"*You* have done well, good and faithful
Servant," He seemed to say. "And
You will continue."

I was helped at last
To the blessing of myself,
It was all that mattered.

A Prayer
For One Who Is Depressed

Dear God, I am tired. How tired I am. But, tired or not, I have life's journey to travel. I am not a very good traveler. I can't even seem to get started. I worry about so much and accomplish so little. Help me, Lord. Give me a social "image" that is workable. The one I have is much too big. It tortures me so that I cannot live within myself. Lord, help me with my panic and rage. I don't want them, but they are there like wolves ready to devour me.

Lord, you see how troubled I am. I need hope. Help me to surface the powers of hope I have within me. Help me, Lord. I can do what I must to get better if I know you are with me. How silly I am. Of course you are with me. Anyway, help me, Lord, to help myself. I am counting on your help. I know you won't disappoint me.

Amen

Other publications by Russell Abata, C.SS.R.

You and the Ten Commandments
Series of nine booklets — *$7.95*

Sexual Morality
$1.50

How to Develop a Better Self-image
$2.50

Helps for the Scrupulous
$2.50

Other helpful publications from Liguori

Five Remedies for Worry
How to Check Your Anger
Nine Keys to Mental Health
Tension: How to Cope with It
Tranquillity without Tranquilizers
What's Wrong with Getting Angry?
What to Do if You're Depressed

35¢ each